8
ESSENTIAL
EXCHANGES

8

ESSENTIAL EXCHANGES

WHAT YOU HAVE TO GIVE UP TO GO UP

KEVIN PAUL SCOTT

What people are saying about 8 Essential Exchanges...

"In *8 Essential Exchanges,* Kevin Paul Scott successfully challenges, encourages and inspires us. His book will shake you out of mediocrity and into a life that truly matters. He has finally captured—and is sharing on paper—what he has been passionately communicating to audiences in person."

Mark Richt
Head Football Coach at the University of Georgia

"The poet Mary Oliver ends one of her poems with the line, 'Tell me what is it you plan to do with your one wild and precious life.' In his book, *8 Essential Exchanges,* Kevin Scott inspires us to make those essential choices that will make our 'one wild and precious life' one that truly matters. Simply put, this wise and wonderful book will change the way you look at yourself and your world."

Dr. Betty L. Siegel
President Emeritus of Kennesaw State University and longest serving female president of a state university in the United States

"A great part of my personal mission statement revolves around making 'The Great Exchanges' in life. We exchange our limited plans for an even greater plan that transports us to a level we've never experienced before. My great friend, Kevin Scott, puts this principle and many others to work in his first book, *8 Essential Exchanges.* Kevin shows you the power behind making wise trade-offs—choices that set the champions apart from contenders in the game of life. If I were you, I wouldn't miss the opportunity to learn and apply the wisdom from this terrific book!"

Dr. Ike Reighard
CEO of MUST Ministries, Senior Pastor of Piedmont Church, and co-author of Daily Insights with Zig Ziglar

"Through stories, insights, quotes, and personal applications, Kevin Scott gives guidance on the most important decisions of our lives. *8 Essential Exchanges* is a great book that I will add to my leadership library."

Nancy Blythe
Chief Talent Officer, Walton Communities

"Don't let the good become the enemy of the best in your life. Follow Kevin's advice and example to build an extraordinary life. Live your life on purpose—make the 8 *Essential Exchanges*. Kevin's book can be your roadmap for an extraordinary life!"

Mark Miller
Vice President of Organizational Effectiveness at Chick-fil-A,
Bestselling Author and Founder of GreatLeadersServe.org
@LeadersServe

"Kevin Scott is a young man who makes a great first impression. After you get to know him, you realize your first impression was 'spot-on!' Central to the understanding of leadership is that life is filled with trade-offs, or as Kevin calls them, 'exchanges.' Rising to new levels of leadership requires sacrifice and selflessness. That's reality—and it's what Kevin explains so well in this book."

Dr. John Hull
Global CEO of The Crossroads Communications Group

"In 8 *Essential Exchanges*, Kevin Scott presents timeless truths in a clear and compelling way. I believe these principles have the power to change your life. I have known Kevin for nearly a decade, traveled with him to Africa, Europe, and Cuba, and listened to him speak to leaders at all levels. I admire Kevin, appreciate his friendship and am proud of his refreshing perspective on life and leadership."

Vince Dooley
Legendary University of Georgia Coach, former Athletic
Director, and member of the College Football Hall of Fame

"Everyone wants a life of meaning and impact, but too few of us stop long enough to fulfill this desire or create a plan to achieve it. We trudge through each day wondering why our lives are so hectic and hoping things will magically calm down. In 8 *Essential Exchanges*, Kevin gives us a clear-cut way of thinking through important choices. So stop, take a deep breath, and read this book with optimism, knowing you can experience the true meaning of life and positively influence the lives of others along the way."

Allison Ausband
Vice President, Reservation Sales & Customer Care, Delta Air Lines

"I absolutely love the concept of this book. I have been in leadership for 28 years in every country of the Western hemisphere, and my experience tells me that Kevin hit the nail on the head with 8 *Essential Exchanges*. Most people never live their dream or reach their maximum potential, not because they aren't gifted or because their dream isn't a worthy one, but because they aren't willing to make the exchanges that will place them on a course of greatness. Kevin shows us the way."

Juan Vereecken
President of Lidere Inc. and Founder Vida Internacional, Mexico

"All of life is a trade-off. When I left India and made the United States my home, that was a trade-off. And every 'yes' is pregnant with a 'no.' When I accept one invitation, it means saying 'no' to another on the same date and time. In 8 *Essential Exchanges*, Kevin Scott will help you understand this crucial principle, find pathways to implementing it, and enjoy the rich dividends of those exchanges. The book you hold in your hand could be transformational . . . are you ready?"

Dr. Samuel R. Chand
Leadership Consultant and Author of Cracking Your Church's Culture Code (*www.samchand.com*)

"Kevin has an uncanny instinct to identify when and how to leverage the seemingly counterintuitive in order to spur change. Throughout this book, he shares a tangible roadmap for anyone who wants to achieve the global successes he's enjoyed."

Gary Whitehill
Founder of New York Entrepreneur Week

Jacket design by Lindsay Miller, Atlanta, Georgia
Interior formatting by Anne McLaughlin, Blue Lake Design
ISBN: 978-1-888237-95-5
Published by Baxter Press, Friendswood, Texas
Second Printing 2015
Printed in the United States

❧

This book is dedicated to my parents, Jeff and Lynne Scott,
who made the essential exchanges to create a great life
for my sister and me.

CONTENTS

THE NATURE OF EXCHANGES

"Our greatest fear should not be of failure,
but of succeeding at things in life that don't really matter."
—Francis Chan

I never saw an activity I wanted to turn down. From the time I was a kid, I wanted to join every organization, club, and sports team. As a student at the University of Georgia, I was involved in political causes, ministries, charities, clubs, and sports. I wanted to fit in, to feel included, and to impress people, so I couldn't say "no" to anything or anyone. I watched *SportsCenter* almost every night so I could talk intelligently with my friends who loved football, baseball, and basketball as much as I did.

My university classes were simply a backdrop for my busy life. Studying seemed like a waste of time, so I learned how to game the system. I did just enough to maintain a respectable (but certainly not impressive) GPA. I looked for courses that credited homework as only ten percent of the final grade. I could make an 87 in the class without doing any homework, and I was completely happy with a B.

I was on campus all the time, involved in various activities, but I skipped class frequently. Being at the university gave me an incredible range of opportunities to do the things I wanted to do. I didn't realize it, but I had a problem: my involvement was a mile wide, but it was only an inch deep.

When I discovered that the charities on campus were full of attractive coeds, I suddenly became interested in those organizations. It wasn't that I had my eye on a particular girl, but the idea of hanging around a lot of them was alluring.

Through a mutual friend, I met Grant Zarzour. He encouraged me to get involved with a specific organization he recommended. Grant said, "Kevin, you've got to join. You'll love this group! It's helping kids who are affected by HIV/AIDS."

The charity was UGA HEROs. The acronym stands for "Hearts Everywhere Reaching Out." At the time I knew very little about the issues facing kids with the disease, and in fact, I didn't think many kids in Georgia were affected. I associated AIDS with pictures of orphaned children in Africa.

To be honest, I wasn't interested.

But Grant told me there were two other good reasons to get involved. To begin with, a couple of football coaches were heavily involved: Georgia's legendary coach, Vince Dooley, and the current head coach, Mark Richt. Grant promised, "If you get involved, you'll get to hang out with both of those men." I had seen them plenty of times on ESPN and from the stands, but getting to know them personally would be really special. I also found out that 80 percent of the college students involved in the organization were girls. Famous football coaches and pretty girls—it doesn't get any better than that! Grant was quite the salesman, and I couldn't refuse.

After I got to know the people in the organization and saw the needs in the kids' lives, my heart melted. I had no idea the disease had devastated the lives of so many children in Georgia's cities and towns. Before long, my motivation to participate deepened and broadened.

UGA HEROs wasn't my only interest at the university. I participated in many other student groups, and even dabbled in politics. For some reason, I've always found the political process appealing. I enjoyed the challenge of thinking deeply about complex issues and then finding a way to articulate those ideas to change people's minds. I spent time with other students who thought and believed like I did, and together, we wanted to make a difference. My passion for politics certainly wasn't genetic. My parents always voted, but they weren't particularly partisan.

CAPTURED

I thoroughly enjoyed everything I was doing. I had a lot of relationships and was always busy doing positive things, but I wasn't really making a difference. As I got more involved in UGA HEROs, I faced a turn-

> I realized there is a difference between believing something is true and having that truth capture your heart.

ing point. I realized there is a difference between believing something is true and having that truth capture your heart. For instance, I may read a report that the manatees in Florida are endangered, but I don't care enough to do anything about it. In the same way, I had seen innumerable news reports and read countless articles about the ravages of AIDS, but I hadn't lifted a finger to help relieve the suffering . . . until I spent time with kids and their parents whose lives were shattered by the sickness.

I had made some important (and negative) assumptions about children with AIDS, but I discovered that those kids weren't suffering because they had made foolish choices. They were innocent victims, not fools or criminals. I was also stunned to discover that Georgia has the second highest rate of pediatric AIDS cases in the entire United States, behind only New York. Most of the kids our charity tried to help lived in households with an annual income of under $10,000, and half of them had lost one or both parents to HIV/AIDS. Those were merely sterile facts, though, until I met some of the children.

The charity sponsored an annual event called "Film on the Fifty." Sports Illustrated called it one of the 100 "must do" events on a college campus. One day each year we turned the University of Georgia football stadium into one of the largest movie theaters in the world. (Sanford Stadium holds more than 92,000 people.) Buses brought kids from all over the state—and especially from the cities—to Athens to spend a day with college students. We gathered the children on the field, "between the hedges," and showed *The Incredibles* on the JumboTron.

I was really excited about the event. I was sure the kids would love the movie, but actually, they couldn't have cared less. We thought they would be in awe to be in one of the most prestigious stadiums in the country. It didn't matter to them at all. The look on their faces told us something mattered more than the film or the place. Those kids were thrilled to be hanging out with college students who cared about them. The children simply wanted someone to call a friend. It was more about the relationships, not the entertainment.

That day my group spent time with a six-year-old girl, Sarah, who lived with her grandmother because both her parents had died from AIDS. She was adorable. The thing that most excited her was something most of us take for granted. After the movie, HERO provided food for the children. When Sarah found out Chick-fil-A sandwiches were going to be served, she looked at us with her big brown eyes and said, "Chick-fil-A is my favorite food in the whole world, but I never get to eat it."

We made sure Sarah was at the front of the line. We got her a sandwich and walked back to the center of the football field to sit down to eat. Brie, one of the girls in our group, cut the sandwich in half for her so it would be easier to eat. Sarah quickly ate the first half, and then she wrapped up the other half. We were confused and asked her, "I thought Chick-fil-A was your favorite. Don't you want to finish the sandwich?"

She responded, "I do. But I really want to save it for my grandmother at home who never gets to have Chick-fil-A either."

At that moment, I realized how incredibly selfish I had been my whole life. This little girl had a life of tragic loss and poverty, but she thought of her grandmother instead of herself. I spent my days thinking mostly about me—my comfort, my enjoyment, and my reputation. When I saw the immensity of her generosity toward her grandmother, I suddenly felt very, very small. I made an immediate dramatic shift from just knowing about an issue to actually caring about the people affected by it.

Another HERO event further melted and molded my heart. A bunch of college students attended a fun field day event for children in Atlanta. The final activity of the day involved kids writing their wishes on helium-filled balloons and then releasing them into the sky. Many of the kids wrote that they wanted to become rappers or doctors or NBA basketball stars. However, some of the other responses will stick with me forever. A fourteen-year-old boy wrote, "I wish I could graduate from high school." His ten-year-old brother scribbled, "I just wish my family would be all right." I watched as a little girl wrote, "I ♥ God. I just wish God ♥d me."

At that moment, my myriad involvements in good but superficial activities looked very insignificant. From the experience with the Chick-fil-A sandwich, I realized how small I was. From the little girl's message on the balloon, I realized I had a bigger purpose than I had ever dreamed possible. I realized my driving purpose from that point on would be to leverage my life to restore hope to people who had lost it. I have an opportunity—and an obligation—to make a difference in the lives of people who desperately need help.

Worth the Trade

Our lives are full of exchanges—or at least, opportunities for exchange. Every choice, including avoiding a choice, is a value statement. Our minds focus on the things that seem most important to us. It might be pleasure, comfort, wealth, power, acceptance, control, or prestige. Whatever it is, we try to accumulate it. The habit begins in childhood. For instance, many girls I know went through the Beanie Babies craze. They started collecting dozens of the tiny stuffed animals, and soon they couldn't live without this one or that one. Children and adults alike would search fervently for any remaining prized Babies they wanted for their collection.

For many boys like me, baseball cards were an obsession. The card I and all the other ten-year-olds wanted—but few had—was the 1989 Upper Deck Ken Griffey Jr. rookie card. All card collectors know there are three ways to get the card you are looking for: (1) you can buy hundreds of packs of cards and hope one of them contains the card you want; (2) you can go to a store and pay a premium for that particular card in a plastic case; or (3) you can trade for it. I didn't have faith that I could buy enough packs from 1989 to discover the Holy Grail inside one of them, so the first option was out. My parents knew how badly I wanted that card, but they weren't going to spend a lot of money on a little piece of cardboard. So I had only one option left. I had to figure out what I could trade one of my friends for it. I had to put a package together—a group of outstanding players in their prime—if I had any hope of convincing the owner of a Ken Griffey Jr. rookie card to part with it. I had to give up some thing, or things, of value to get something of equal or greater value in return. I couldn't just pull a random card of an unknown backup shortstop out of my box and expect to trade it for a Ken Griffey Jr.

Choices between good and bad decisions are usually easy to make. Most people aren't struggling to decide between becoming a drug dealer or starting a business, between murdering someone or marrying them, between cooking meth or serving the poor in the inner city. When I speak of making important exchanges, I'm referring to choices between really good things and even better things. Those are much harder to make, but they shape our lives in disproportionate ways.

In this book we will take a hard look at the exchanges that really matter—the ones that take you beyond an average, nice, comfortable life into one that is full of challenge, meaning, and impact. In the chapters that follow, I will challenge you to exchange:

- stability for significance;
- fans for friends;
- dollars for difference;
- expedience for excellence;
- shifting sands for a solid rock;
- being the master of none to being the master of one;
- acceptance for accomplishment; and
- the immediate for the ultimate.

> If you find the courage to make those choices, you will certainly face some internal conflict and external opposition, but it will be worth it.

These are the exchanges I have chosen to make (and I have to keep making). I have watched others make similar hard, but necessary, choices. Other authors and speakers may suggest more, or fewer, exchanges, but the number and the exact wording aren't important. The crucial thing is to clearly identify the most important choices of your life. If you find the courage to make those choices, you will certainly face some internal conflict and external opposition, but it will be worth it. You will enjoy more happiness and fulfillment than you ever imagined, and you will find the best friends of your life.

To be honest, some of these exchanges have been relatively easy for me, but others are excruciatingly difficult. Life isn't stagnant or predictable. At different points, we might face the same exchanges at deeper levels, or we may face new ones. At such significant moments, we have a tendency to drift back toward the comfortable, the stable, and the familiar.

You don't have to be a wild-eyed visionary to make dramatic exchanges. They're common to every person on the planet. Different personalities, though, handle them in different ways. Some of us are natural risk-takers, and others are cautious. In our own way, all of us face the thrill and the threat of exchanges, and for all of us it requires clear thinking and courage. I'm not suggesting that you will do it perfectly. You will try and fail. You will get confused and go off track. There are few guarantees, but that's part of the thrill of a life well lived.

The Ken Griffey Jr. rookie card symbolizes the best things in every aspect of my life: my career, family, and friendships. If I want the best, I have to give up some really good things, and we dare not paint good things as wrong in order to make the decisions easier. It cost plenty to get Ken Griffey Jr.'s rookie card because the other cards I had to give up weren't worthless. In the same way, we may feel a loss when we exchange good things for something even better.

My Hope for You

As you read about the eight exchanges in this book, I hope there are times when you think, "Wow, I never thought about that before!" And I hope you find the courage to make new choices—not all at once, but when the time is right for each one. A comfortable, easy life has some benefits, but it can't bring genuine fulfillment. I believe we've been created to live for something much bigger than our entertainment and happiness. Our lives can really matter. Each of these exchanges takes us a step closer to getting up every morning with the certainty that our lives count.

As I have watched and worked with others, I've noticed a methodology that works in every exchange: *engage, expose,* and *equip.* My experience with UGA HEROs is a good example. I *engaged* in the organization for self-absorbed reasons—football and girls. Those motivations resonated with me at that point in my life, but they were just a step on the road. When I got more involved, I was *exposed* to needs, hopes, and hurts in a way that shook me out of my complacency and shifted the way that I saw the world. Then, through the organization, I was *equipped* with a platform and the tools to make a difference in the lives of those children who so desperately needed some hope and some help.

This pattern is thoroughly transferable. No matter where we go or what we do, we can engage people where they are, expose them more deeply to the needs of others, and then equip them to meet those needs in specific, tangible ways. I hope you see this process as you apply each of the exchanges to your own life . . . and as you lead and encourage others.

Whenever we wrestle with challenging new choices, most of us need some encouragement along the way. Very few people are fiercely independent entrepreneurs who are comfortable facing the most daunting obstacles alone. The majority of us wilt under such pressure. We are created with the need to give and receive support. Our exchanges force us to look at our most deeply held beliefs, the foundation of our security, and our most cherished dreams. It's very easy to take a quick look, shake our heads, and walk away. We need someone—a mentor, a friend, a partner, a parent—who will cheer when we show some courage, hug us when we fail, and give us a kick in the butt when we're reluctant to take a necessary step.

I was fortunate to have the encouragement of parents who are tenacious optimists and supported every step I have taken. I wouldn't have gotten far without their consistent love and reassurance. I have had wonderful role models, including Coach Vince Dooley and Garrett Gravesen, my friend and business partner who has pushed me, inspired me, and challenged me to always take one more step.

Some books are written for people with advanced degrees who are well along their career path, make a substantial salary, and have a wealth of resources. This book, though,

> The exchanges apply to everyone of every age at every income level in every culture.

isn't limited to any particular demographic group. The exchanges apply to everyone of every age at every income level in every culture. The opportunities are unlimited.

Making exchanges can be both uncomfortable and thrilling. Many of us have carefully crafted our lives to remain as comfortable as possible. I hope this book nudges you to take an honest look at your goals, realize where they're leading, and make the necessary exchanges that all of us ought to make.

Real life and genuine fulfillment take place outside your comfort zone. If you insist on remaining comfortable, the concepts in this book will seem foolish to you. But if you're willing to be challenged, you might discover more thrills than you ever imagined.

8

Chapter 1

Exchanging Stability
for Significance

*"Really, it comes down to your philosophy. Do you want to play it safe and
be good, or do you want to take a chance and be great?"*
—Jimmy Johnson, NASCAR driver

I know a few people who live for an adrenaline rush. The greater the risk, the greater the pleasure. They live to BASE jump, ride 40-foot waves at Mavericks, or wrestle alligators with their bare hands. Those people are in a different category from most of the rest of humanity, who has a healthy respect for stability. The problem is that we can value stability too much.

One of the highest honors awarded at the University of Georgia is the selection of a student commencement speaker for graduation. When I was a senior, they picked me. I was really surprised and deeply honored. In fact, some people who had known me since I was a boy were *very* surprised. I wasn't a star student. I was simply with the right people at the right time with the right cause. Those in charge of the commencement ceremony allotted seven minutes for my talk. They threatened to throw a rope over me and drag me off the stage if I went too long. Either they didn't want to look foolish, or they were happy for me to look foolish, because I finally sat down after speaking for more than 14 minutes.

The honor looked good on my résumé and led to a lot of job offers. I began working for a national candidate during the primary season of the 2008 presidential campaign. I became the college campus co-ordinator for my state, and ultimately, I traveled to several states to rally college students to support the individual I represented. I spoke to political groups on campuses and wrote op-ed pieces for school newspapers. The challenge was stimulating, and I was especially passionate about it because I was working for someone I believed in. I was convinced my candidate was the right person to lead our country.

That individual, however, lost in the primaries, so I needed to find something else to do. The campaign had helped me realize that working in politics could never be just a job for me. I truly had to believe that whomever I supported was the very best choice for the position. I couldn't settle for being a political operative who sold my services to whoever would pay me. I had to drink the Kool-Aid. I had to be all in.

While I was absorbed in the campaign, a couple of my friends had begun laying the groundwork for an organization designed to change the way students see the world. Many universities already conducted study abroad programs, but my friends and I had come to the conclusion that a lot of those programs were lacking.

About 250,000 students travel to other countries for short periods of time—and sometimes, whole semesters—yet their experiences are rarely transformative. Many (if not most) American students who study in other countries end up spending most of their time in class-rooms that look an awful lot like the ones they sit in back in the states. Students often traveled halfway across the world to sit in a classroom five or six hours a day, four or five days a week, and then spent all of their free time partying. The only culture they experienced was in the clubs.

On the other hand, a small percentage of students engage in mission programs that give them a chance to build homes, teach children, feed the hungry, and meet all kinds of other needs. Such programs are great, but they don't attract nearly as many students, largely because no college credit is given.

My friends and I began to reimagine the formal study abroad programs. If we could blend the best of the existing college programs with the best of missions trips—lots of fun and excitement, along with course credit and meaningful connections to the local culture—how could students' lives be changed? In addition, we dreamed of exposing students to the very best leaders in the world, men and women who would inspire them to dream big dreams and never settle for a comfortable but meaningless life. The plan was to create a unique environment that would change the way students look at the world and their role in touching lives.

If we could create life-changing, catalytic study abroad programs, students would return with bigger, better ideas for how they could make a difference. Some might choose to devote themselves to another culture for the rest of their lives, but many more would come back to America to be better husbands, wives, fathers, mothers, doctors, business people, pastors, lawyers, and citizens of every kind.

My friends invited me to join them on the journey and be a part of the team. I was thrilled with their plans and strategy, but I had two problems. First, I knew absolutely nothing about cultures around the world. I had never traveled outside the country, and I didn't even have a passport. The second problem was even more critical. The organization wouldn't launch until September, but it was March and I was unemployed. I needed a job, and I needed one fast.

Due to my work on the presidential campaign, I was able to land a job as a field representative for a United States Congressman. My job was to meet with local constituents to connect them with the policies in Washington. I was the congressman's earpiece to tell him what the people in the district thought and felt about issues, and I was the mouthpiece to communicate relevant events and policies back to the people.

The presidential campaign had been thrilling because it was full of risks and potential rewards for the country. I had stayed awake many nights and I drank a lot of Red Bull to keep going. Working for the congressman was also glamorous. I had two offices, one in the city and one in the mountains of Georgia. I was just out of college, but either of my offices would have been the envy of partners in prestigious law firms. In both locations I had fine desks flanked by flags, an array of artwork, and comfy couches. I had interns who reported to me, and civic leaders from across the district called me. Sometimes I had to pinch myself. I had incredible connections, opportunities, a sizeable paycheck, a car, and a nice apartment. I was just out of school, but I had arrived!

My new job enabled me to do a lot of really fun things, but there wasn't much risk. It was very safe. And I can't pinpoint the exact moment, but sometime during those months I started thinking, *This job is pretty sweet. Maybe I'll keep doing this instead of launching a new kind of leadership-focused study abroad program with my friends.* I was feeling comfortable . . . very comfortable.

After a few months on the job, an important event took place at the Classic Center in Athens, Georgia. Every four years, the living secretaries of state hold a gathering to offer bipartisan advice to the incoming administration. The congressman I worked for couldn't attend, so I went in his place. The former secretaries who were present that year were Colin Powell, Madeleine Albright, Henry Kissinger, James Baker, and Warren Christopher. I sat next to Secretary Albright at lunch. A photographer snapped a picture of me with my arm around her. The two of us talked for an hour about the conflicts and political turmoil around the globe. When the five former secretaries gathered for a group picture, I photobombed them!

When the meeting was over, I sent a lot of my friends an email with a picture of me with the secretaries. The subject line read: "Just another day at the office." I was so full of myself that I simply couldn't keep it in!

The next morning I had breakfast with my Mom and Dad at a Waffle House. The contrast between that setting and the previous day's couldn't have been starker. I couldn't wait to tell them about my lunch with the Secretaries of State, and they were thrilled to hear my stories. They seemed to enjoy my telling them how great I was . . . in the way loving and proud parents would.

When we finished eating, my dad got up to go to work. He's a firefighter, and he had on his blue uniform with his name above the breast pocket. As he got into his fire-engine-red pickup truck and drove away, it struck me that as long as I could remember, my father had worked 24 hours on and 48 hours off. On the days he wasn't at the station, he worked in his own construction business. Sometimes he would be up all night fighting a fire, and when he got home he would go straight to a construction site to saw lumber and swing a hammer the rest of the day.

Those days, he might work until 7:00 p.m., but he still came to my Little League baseball games.

That's when it hit me: My father had devoted his life to serve people and make a difference in their lives. He does something that matters. His work isn't glamorous, and he doesn't make a lot of money, but it's what he loves to do. As a firefighter, he risks his life for others—and he has never made a big deal about it. He could have chosen a safer job during those 30 years, but to him the risk was worth the opportunity to have a positive—even lifesaving—impact on others. After breakfast I would be going back to a job where people thought I was important, but suddenly, that seemed very empty. *I* wanted a job where *the impact* was important, no matter what anyone thought of me.

> My father had devoted his life to serve people and make a difference in their lives. He does something that matters.

Driving to my office, I pondered the last few months as my thoughts swirled. I felt very fulfilled in college because I worked with a charity that helped overlooked and needy children. In the presidential campaign, I was energized because I believed my candidate could have a positive impact on our nation and the world. Those roles involved risks, and they kept me awake at night with anticipation. My current job with the congressman had far more perks, but it was safe—very safe. It wasn't challenging, it didn't bring out the best in me, and I wasn't really making much of a difference (except in my ability to brag about a cool photo).

It was during that drive when I decided to exchange security and stability for the opportunity to join my friends in the risky venture of starting a new organization. The first item on the agenda? Spending one hundred days traveling through Africa.

Going overseas for extended periods sounds like fun, but it meant leaving the comfort, prestige, and financial stability of a job back home to work long hours and make little or no money in the foreseeable future. It meant leaving two fancy offices with the latest technology to start "officing" in coffee shops so I could use their Internet. It also meant giving up my apartment and moving back in with my parents. (For the record, the best way to get a girlfriend is not by living with your parents!)

I was well aware that all those sacrifices were part of the deal if I joined my friends in their efforts to create a new way for students to see, serve, and study abroad. For all we knew, the idea might not even work. Then we would be unemployed and broke, with failure on our résumés. There were absolutely no guarantees.

STABILITY PROMISES ...

Most of us feel very uncomfortable with uncertainty. To a great degree, human beings are creatures of habit. Life would be unworkable if too many things were up for grabs in our lives. Chaos isn't a goal, and insanity isn't a strategy. Even daring people who climb Mount Everest or start companies need a certain measure of stability, and on the continuum of security and risk, most of us lean very strongly toward the predictable.

Since the time of the ancient Greeks, scholars have identified several different personality types. Each type has a unique approach to risk and stability. Some have never seen a risk they didn't like. Such people will go anywhere and do anything for the sake of excitement. Not many people are like this, but they're often the most interesting ones in the room. To be honest, many of them don't care as much about the activity as the rush of adrenaline it provides. To their credit, I believe most risk-takers are very selective. They may thrive on risk, yet they don't take risks in every part of their lives. Some risk their finances, but not their health or relationships. Others will move to the other side of the world and start new relationships, but they won't take any risks with their finances. Whether the risk is in sports, careers, or another part of life, everything else is off limits. When we look at those people, we don't find a single profile—except a high tolerance for risk of some kind.

On the other end of the spectrum are those who are risk-averse. They want everything nailed down before they are willing to make a move. Maybe they've been burned in the past and have become cautious, or perhaps the need for stability was modeled for them when they were children. Such people have difficulty making a decision until they've explored every option and analyzed every possible outcome. Whatever the case, stability is their highest value.

Risk isn't inherently right or wrong. Neither is stability. We can be foolish or fearful on either side of the equation. However, when the enticement of stability gets in the way of doing something that's challenging and fulfilling, we need to make an adjustment—we need to make an exchange. Ultimately, meaning trumps stability.

When we sacrifice fulfillment for security, we settle for less than the purpose for which we were created. We can observe people from different cultures, different ethnicities, different economic groups, different religions, and different ages, and at the core of them all is the desire for their lives to count for something bigger than themselves. It's built in, standard equipment for human beings.

At crucial points in our careers and relationships, we face an important choice: will we exchange the potential gain of fulfillment for safety and stability? The question is seldom simple. As each opportunity arises, we have to weigh the potential for significance and impact. Sometimes it may not be worth taking the risk, but many times security is a poor consolation prize if you give up the chance to make a difference.

> When we sacrifice fulfillment for security, we settle for less than the purpose for which we were created.

Most of us have a very clear picture of the way life should be. We don't anticipate living like Jay-Z and Beyoncé, but we do expect to have enough friends, enough money, enough career prestige, enough time to do the things we want to do, and enough protection against failure. The American dream is that our lives and our possessions will keep growing—always moving up and to the right on the chart. We're sure we will soon have bigger and nicer stuff, more and better friends, and more time to enjoy it all—an increasingly comfortable life. Our pursuit of happiness seems completely reasonable and right—because everyone we know is chasing the same things! The promise, though, is an empty one. Eventually a comfortable lifestyle leaves us empty, confused, and living on a treadmill, chasing more of the things that can't ultimately satisfy. A lot of people wake up one day and wonder why their lives are so unbearably dull. Older people tell me that's what a midlife crisis is about. It is wise to make changes long before we get to that point.

Comparison drives people to strive to acquire more—more money, power, prestige, and possessions. It takes insight and courage to get off that treadmill.

Authors Joseph Heller (*Catch-22*) and Kurt Vonnegut (*Slaughter-house Five*) were good friends. Vonnegut told an insightful story about Heller at the 1998 Rice University commencement address, and repeated it after Heller's death in an article in the *New Yorker*. Here is what he wrote:

> Joseph Heller, an important and funny writer now dead, and I were at a party given by a billionaire on Shelter Island.
>
> I said, "Joe, how does it make you feel to know that our host only yesterday may have made more money than your novel *Catch-22* has earned in its entire history?"
>
> And Joe said, "I've got something he can never have."
>
> And I said, "What on earth could that be, Joe?"
>
> And Joe said, "The knowledge that I've got enough."[1]

Heller is the exception. Most people never get enough. They are more like John D. Rockefeller, the founder and president of Standard Oil, and in his day, the richest man in the world. In an interview, a reporter asked, "Mr. Rockefeller, how much money is enough money?"

The oil baron replied, "Just a little bit more."[2]

The problem with valuing stability more than significance is that we're chasing a moving target. No matter how much wealth, fame, beauty, or power we get, someone else always has more. When we reach a goal in those areas, it feels great—but only for a short while. Soon the glory wears off. We look around and realize there are many more rungs on the ladder. We see people who are richer, smarter, more handsome or beautiful, and more popular, and we can't rest until we climb the next rung.

In a variation on pursuing the American dream, many people plan to find and fulfill their dreams, but later . . . *after* they have provided comfort and stability as a platform for their futures. The plan sounds reasonable, but quite often the acquisition of money and possessions gradually (or not so gradually) consumes the person's heart. Before long, the dream dies from neglect. The only thing remaining is the false promise that acquiring more stuff will someday bring true fulfillment. It won't. It can't. We're not wired that way.

FACING OUR FEARS

For many of us, the core problem is the fear of losing control. We simply aren't willing to take our hands off the steering wheel of our lives in order to devote ourselves to something that captures our hearts and then see what happens. We can point to people who tried great things and failed miserably, and we conclude, "I don't want to end up like them!" We don't want to risk looking foolish, being the brunt of jokes or the object of whispers, or losing opportunities while we chase our dreams.

To be honest, one of my fears when I dove into the new venture to re-create study abroad programs was that I would miss something I dearly love—college football games. That may sound trivial to some people, but those people are obviously not college football fans! Our team traveled in Africa for three months during the heart of the football season, so I got to see only one game that year. We found a hotel bar with ESPN, and we watched the game at 3:00 in the morning. It was fun, but it reminded me of all the other games I didn't get to see. Missing the season was a cost I had to pay, and I didn't like paying it.

Our fears are frequently disguised by what often appear to be perfectly *reasonable* conclusions. After all, we want to be responsible people. When we face an exchange of stability to gain significance, we

> Our fears are frequently disguised by what often appear to be perfectly reasonable conclusions.

might shrug and say, "Well, that would be great, but I have to take care of [fill in the blank]." We point to our jobs, our parents' health, our college debts, and a dozen other important things. Some of those, maybe all of them, are genuine *responsibilities*, but they may also be excuses rather than actual *roadblocks*.

If you have a dream, and you devote creative energies to finding a way to follow that dream, you can usually find a way to meet your obligations and still do what enflames your heart. Too often, so-called responsibilities are our first line of retreat. They're convenient, they make sense, and people have a hard time arguing with us.

But I'll argue with you. Don't use phantom responsibilities as an excuse, and don't let actual responsibilities be a roadblock. Find a way to follow your dream.

Every decision to pursue an opportunity has a cost. A choice to do one thing automatically eliminates an infinite number of other options. Young adults today value keeping their options open, often to the point of sacrificing the risk required to follow their hearts.

When I speak to audiences, I often explain that any bold choice to make a difference gives us more of two things in life and less of another one. Such decisions increase our responsibilities because we take ownership of a goal, and they raise our *ability to have a profound influence on people*. At the same time they automatically and dramatically *limit our options*. This is an inevitable result of making exchanges, and for some, the fear of having fewer opportunities is a serious barrier.

Fear is a straightjacket. In his book, *A Million Miles in a Thousand Years*, Donald Miller communicated a significant insight about the power of fear: "Before I realized we were supposed to fight fear, I thought of fear as a subtle suggestion in our subconscious designed to keep us safe, or more important, keep us from getting humiliated. And I guess it serves that purpose. But fear isn't only a guide to keep us safe; it's also a manipulative emotion that can trick us into living a boring life."[3]

Some of us have lived without a compelling challenge for a long time. We graduated from college, landed a job, and got married, but we've been coasting from one comfortable decision to another. Big dreams, it seems, are for "those people." But it doesn't have to stay that way. All of us are made for something that challenges and inspires us. We need to find whatever it is and invest our lives in fulfilling it. If you've given up on having a dream like that, dream again. It's never too late. If you have a pulse, you have a purpose.

I'm not suggesting we give up stability as an end in itself. That's foolish. Rather, I'm asking us to use a different matrix to make important choices. Instead of putting security and safety at the top of our priority list, we need to replace those values with another one: the chance to have a significant impact on others. We may make less money, we may feel uncomfortable, and our friends may drive nicer cars and live in bigger houses, but we can have a categorically different priority at the top of our list.

WORTH THE RISK

When my life was a mile wide and an inch deep, I kept all my options open. I had a lot of fun, but I didn't have much of an impact on people. After graduating from college, I had what many people considered a dream job, but it didn't capture my heart. It gave me comfort and prestige, but didn't challenge me to live for a greater cause. At the points when I have walked away from comfort to embrace a dream, it has been scary, but worth it. Things haven't always gone smoothly. Adventures don't work like that! They're full of unknowns, plot twists, and surprising characters, but I would much rather live in a thrilling drama than a self-absorbed soap opera.

One of the things I cherish is knowing I have been able to make a difference in the lives of hurting people. I have loved it, and I don't ever want to settle for less. I want to leverage comfort, certainty, and every resource I have to make a lasting and positive impact.

When we launched the new study abroad program in 2008, four of us embarked on a reconnaissance mission, a 100-day trip from Kenya to Cape Town, South Africa. We began in Kenya because Garrett, my friend who founded HERO, got his inspiration from working with HIV/AIDS orphans in that country. It was thrilling to walk onto the grounds of the orphanage where his vision began. I had worked with children in Georgia, but the genesis of that organization came from this plot of ground in Kenya and the faces of these children. Parts of the trip were difficult for me. I don't know if my friends could tell how uncomfortable I felt. I had never traveled extensively, so everything was new to me: the food, the bathrooms, the beds, the travel, the smells, and the inconvenience.

A year later we took our first group of 50 students to Africa. We traveled to a remote area of South Africa where we lived on a dollar a day, the average wage of a worker in that part of the country, to immerse ourselves in the lives of the people. At Sir Lowry's Pass in the

Hottentots-Holland mountain range, the people of the village were amazed that Americans would want to connect with them.

But the bigger impact on that trip was on the students. One girl was from a very wealthy family. When we went into the township, she was wearing an $800 pair of shoes. Her experience had the kind of impact we hoped it would have. Her heart was broken and remolded by the needs of the people she met. After the program was over, she devoted her life to care for disadvantaged people, and she's making a difference. She has a multiplied impact because many of those she is helping are caring for others, too.

Several of the students who went on our trips are involved in Teach for America, mostly in inner cities. They exchanged comfort and stability to reach out and change the lives of disadvantaged kids. Traveling to a foreign country had revolutionized their worldview. They are willing to make sacrifices wherever they are—to accept narrowed options for the sake of having a greater influence.

I wouldn't trade the experience for anything in the world. I could see the changes taking place in the lives of the students. That's what I hoped for . . . that's what I dreamed would happen. It was incredibly exciting.

How can we determine what to exchange? That's not an easy question. I look at it two ways. First, engage in activities and events that expose you to real needs. Don't be shy. Take the initiative to call an organization or accept a friend's invitation to get involved for a day. You don't have to go to Africa; every community has plenty of unnoticed needs. Charities, churches, and schools often organize regular outreaches to immigrant families, outcasts, the poor, orphans, the elderly, and the homeless. As you expose yourself to a range of needs, your heart will break at some point. That's where you need to invest your time and energy. But be aware that not all organizations are well organized. Some are more of a resource drain than a resource multiplier. Pay attention to people who have been involved for a while. See if they're energized and thrilled, or if you feel like they're wasting their time. Don't stop until you've found a cause and a group of people who stay in your mind and heart even when you're not around them.

The second suggestion takes the opposite approach: Start by taking an inventory of your hopes and dreams, and then acknowledge the fear of losing comfort and stability. What do your dreams promise you? Why do they look so attractive? And what's keeping you from pursuing them? Don't settle for excuses and apathy. Be honest about the phony responsibilities you have used to say "no," and look for ways to fulfill genuine responsibilities while you follow your dream.

You may find that your heart becomes tender at strange times. When we become sensitized to the world around us, things that never bothered us suddenly shatter us. A few years ago, singer Jack Johnson released "The News," a song that describes a mother's attempts to protect her child from the harsh realities during newscasts. She tries to tell her child that the deaths and destruction they see are just make-believe, but she realizes something is missing in the telecast. She asks a piercing question:

> "Why don't the newscasters cry when they read about the people who die?
>
> You'd think they could be decent enough to put just a tear in their eyes."[4]

When we watch the news or read online coverage, we're often exposed to events that have devastated people. Wars, natural disasters, murders, famine, fire, and other events have changed their realities forever, but most of us have become anesthetized to the heartache. The sheer volume of horrible events numbs us. But we need to go there, let

> When we become sensitized to the world around us, things that never bothered us suddenly shatter us.

our hearts be broken, and care for the people we see on the screen. The victims who died in suicide bombings, the women who were raped, the people who were swept away by floods (these were all on the news the day I wrote this)—all of those victims are someone's brother or sister, husband or wife, son or daughter. Those people matter to someone! If we stay disconnected from their reality, our hearts become deadened. If we become sensitive to the pain in the news, we might have to turn it off because it's overwhelming. It's better, though, to be devastated by tragedies than to be entertained by them. It may seem strange to weep when we watch the news, but it's far more appropriate than being numb.

TAKE A STEP

As you become exposed to the needs of people, let the walls of self-protection fall down. Let your heart be disturbed. In fact, consider tears to be a requirement of being fully human. Don't stop looking outward until you clarify your dream, and don't stop looking inward until you've addressed your fears. When that happens, a world of possibilities opens to you. At that point the list of ways to make this exchange is almost endless, from simple and brief options, to investing every dime and minute of your life. For instance, find some friends and take on some of the following commitments.

- Volunteer at a women's shelter, a homeless shelter, or a food pantry.
- Care for a single, pregnant woman.
- Show up to hammer nails on a Habitat for Humanity house.
- Gather supplies for victims of natural disasters.
- Go where the disasters have happened to help people rebuild their homes and their lives.
- Apply to help with a local after-school program.
- Coach a kid's team.
- Go to a nursing home and lead them in singing. Or just hold someone's hand.
- Move from the comfortable suburbs to the city to work, live, and worship.
- Drive your old car another year, take a smaller apartment, go out less often, and give the money you save to a cause you believe in.
- Notice the person who is often left out of lunch gatherings, and invite him or her to eat with you . . . regularly.
- Volunteer to read during story time at a school with disadvantaged kids.
- Build bridges by shopping in stores and eating in restaurants in immigrant neighborhoods.
- Offer your support when you find out someone has a parent who has just died, a spouse with cancer, or a sibling who has left home in anger. Write a letter, make a call, or go and visit to be a shoulder to cry on. Don't feel that you need to provide a lot of answers. Your presence means more than your words.

Some of your friends (or at least people you know from a distance) are great examples of the beauty and benefits that come from exchanging stability for significance. Hang out with them. Ask them to take you with them. See what makes them tick, and see if their passion kindles yours.

As you take steps to exchange stability for significance, one of the biggest benefits will be that you meet some of the most courageous people in the world. Since I've been making this choice, I have met some people who amaze me. One is Paulus Wiratno, a Christian pastor in Indonesia, the most populous Muslim country in the world. Paulus started a Bible school in his community and established 13 orphanages, but Christian groups came under attack from Islamic extremists. In his part of the country, churches were being burned and Christians murdered. His church and school were easy targets.

One night Paulus got a phone call from a man who frantically warned, "They're coming!" Paulus quickly woke his wife, his two daughters, and the 120 students. As they fled into the forest, Paulus carried one of his daughters. His wife struggled to run while carrying the other girl, so she handed her daughter to a student. They all continued to run in the darkness as the flames of the school lit up the night.

Several hours and many miles later, the family and the students stopped to rest. Paulus did a head count to be sure no one was lost. Two were missing: his daughter and the student carrying her. Paulus and a small group left immediately to search for them. Finally, he found them on the bank of a river. His daughter was bleeding and bruised, but she was alive. When he told me this story, he explained the lesson he learned that night: "It's bad to be lost, but it's worse when someone you love is lost." That night he understood far more of God's love for us, and it changed his life and relationships. He became even more committed to share that love with his daughter, of course, but also with the Muslims who tried to kill him, his family, and the students.

Paulus is a man who consistently gives up stability and safety to have the opportunity to touch people, even those who have vowed to kill him. He later told me, "Compassion means you're willing to be disturbed."

How much am I willing to be disturbed?

Sometimes needy, hurting people are under our own roofs. Patrick Henry Hughes was born blind and handicapped, but his father put him in front of a piano when he was only nine months old. The boy turned out to be a musical prodigy. Years later when Patrick was a student at the University of Louisville, the band director invited him to play the trumpet with the marching band as his father pushed him in a wheelchair. The real hero of the story, though, isn't Patrick. It's his dad. To care for his son, John Hughes quit his regular job and took the graveyard shift at UPS. John gave up his career, his financial stability, and his comfort for a higher purpose: to help his son shine like a bright light in the musical world—and to everyone who is inspired by such courage and devotion.

> "Compassion means you're willing to be disturbed."

Some people look at the immensity of the needs they find, and they feel paralyzed. Most of us aren't going to move to Africa to work in orphanages or give all our money to help flood victims in the Philippines. But we can do something. Andy Stanley has suggested a solution: "Do for one what you wish you could do for everyone."[5]

If you're wondering where to start, take one step. You're not committing yourself to a vow of poverty or a lifetime of serving in the slums of Jakarta. You're just taking a step to see if a cause you care about might be worth sacrificing some comfort so you can make an impact. After you take a few steps, it will feel more natural. You're creating a new normal. You'll realize being uncomfortable isn't the worst thing in the world. Living an empty life is far, far worse.

At the end of each chapter, I want to give you a few questions to stimulate your thinking and help you apply the principles. Don't just turn the page and move on to the next chapter. Spend some time with the concepts; let them sink deep into your heart; let the walls fall away. You may discover that something really resonates with you and moves you to take action.

> *"The two most important days in your life are the day you are born and the day you find out why."*
> —Mark Twain

THINK ABOUT IT . . .

Describe a time when you encountered needs in a person's life and you were moved to help in some way. What was the need? How did you help?

What are some reasons (valid or not) that many people choose comfort and stability over significance and impact? Which of those reasons have you used?

What is the next step for you? How will you take it? Who will go with you? What do you hope will happen?

Put Paulus's insight in your own words: "Compassion means you're willing to be disturbed."

8

CHAPTER 2

EXCHANGING FANS FOR FRIENDS

"When people talk, listen completely. Most people never listen."
—Ernest Hemingway

he promise of technology is faster and wider communications. A few years ago the experts told us that cell phones, email, texts, Twitter, Instagram, and all the other tools would deepen our relationships because they provide instant access to people. We certainly have instant access now, but the results have been far different than most expected.

Too often, relationships have become shallower, not deeper. We have become a culture invested in image management instead of creating and developing real friendships. Of course, this observation isn't a universal truth, but it's increasingly true. In our relationships, we need to go far beyond shaping our online identity. We need to find at least a few people who know us—with all of our hopes and hurts. We need to exchange fans for real friends.

Knowing a person's story enables us to feel genuine compassion and respect for him or her. The person's heart is exposed, and we begin to trust. When that happens, we reciprocate—we gradually take off our masks, and our defenses come down. When both people become vulnerable, a meaningful connection can occur. We become more fully human when we are more fully known.

But of course, being vulnerable is risky. If it weren't, we would be completely honest with every person we meet! We don't need a hundred intimate friends, but we need a few. Dr. Brené Brown, a research professor at the University of Houston Graduate College of Social Work, made the threatening but hopeful observation: "What makes you vulnerable makes you beautiful."

Okay, it's time for me to be vulnerable: this is the hardest exchange for me. Everything in me resists exposure. I could learn a lot from my sister. Whitney is open and honest with people. I, on the other hand, would much rather be seen as a leader, the one in charge, the one who has all the answers, the one who doesn't need to depend on anybody. But it is just a pretense, of course. I need people just as much as anyone else, even though I don't *want* to need them. I have a million arm's length friends, but I don't let very many people see behind the mask. It's tough for me to let people get close. It's a struggle I'm continually working on.

My problem is that I'm a people pleaser. You may think that would push me toward deeper relationships, but it doesn't. Those of us who live for approval appear to be highly relational, but if we're not careful, our relationships carry a hidden agenda. We're looking to other people to define our identities, to tell us we have value, and to make us feel secure. The fear is that people will define us as unworthy, less than, and unacceptable, which drives us to try even harder to impress them, make them laugh, and avoid looking stupid. Our greatest fear is disappointing someone. A dis-

> Being a people pleaser certainly drives us toward relationships, but rarely without a mask of competence, friendliness, and humor.

approving look on someone's face crushes us. Being a people pleaser certainly drives us toward relationships, but rarely without a mask of competence, friendliness, and humor.

SHATTERED BY THE TRUTH

All my life I had honed my skills of pleasing people, but I kept others just far enough away to limit the risk of exposing my heart. One day my carefully constructed façade was shattered. Our team took a group of 50 students to Cape Town, South Africa, on our new leadership and service-based study abroad program. Part of our strategy was to expose the students to some of the best leaders we knew. Two people who had impressed and influenced me tremendously were Georgia's former football coach, Vince Dooley, and his wife, Barbara. You might expect Coach Dooley to be the bold, outspoken leader of the two, with Barbara the quiet woman behind the scenes. If that's what you expect, you would be wrong. Barbara Dooley is a firebrand!

The students gathered in a classroom to hear Barbara talk. One side of the room was all windows, and we could see beautiful Table Mountain across the bay in the distance. The title of her message was "The

10 Great Things about Cancer." She had survived the disease, and instead of letting it kill her spirit, she used the ordeal as a steppingstone to learn life's most significant lessons. Struggling with the disease helped her develop deeper relationships, clarified her purpose in life, and freed her from caring as much about other people's opinions. The disease, she explained, had been one of her most valued teachers. When we had scheduled her to speak, I realized the students might never hear anyone else with such a hopeful, positive perspective on suffering. I was thrilled to have them all together in the same room in Cape Town.

Barbara was teaching principles and sharing her heart with the students, and they were eating up every word. It was exactly the kind of experience we wanted to create for the students involved with our program. As usual, I sat in the back of the room with my phone. I was texting people back in the states to let them know what was going on, reading through some emails, and catching up on the news. This was a normal activity for me. I was typically disengaged with what was going on in the room in front of me.

At some point in the middle of her presentation, Barbara stopped talking. I was engrossed in my phone, so I didn't notice . . . until I heard her say in a slightly exasperated tone, "Kevin, what are you doing?"

I looked up, and I saw every face turned toward me. I realized she was calling me out because I was the only person in the room who wasn't fully involved. I wanted to crawl into a hole and hide, but that wasn't an option. She looked at me with a loving but corrective expression. The room was dead silent for a few seconds, which to me seemed like hours. Then she said, "Kevin, wherever you are, be there. Whatever's going on out there can wait. You need to be present with us right now. You're in this place with these people and me. Be here."

I nodded, put my phone down, and paid attention. As a people pleaser, I felt more humiliated than humbled. After thinking about it for a while, however, I realized her words to me meant far more than, "Pay attention." I realized I regularly used disengagement as a defense mechanism to stay aloof from people and appear to have more important things to do.

The next day I had an opportunity to apply the lesson Barbara taught me. We went to a township to work with people who live on about $1 a day. This time I didn't take my phone. I wanted to be all there. A group of us went into a family's home made with corrugated metal for the roof and sheets of thick cardboard for walls. In that little shack, I heard Nicholas tell his story. He was a pastor who would hitchhike 20 miles each week to minister to farmers in an even more remote part of the country. Some days he got a ride all the way, and it didn't take long. But on other days, the trip might take hours as he walked and caught short rides. I was impressed and inspired by this man's devotion to the desperately poor people of the village—and his dear family in that shack.

Suddenly I realized: If I'd had my phone that day, I would have been outside texting friends back at home or setting up the next event, and I would have missed seeing the love on Nicholas's face and hearing the compassion in his voice. Questions flooded my mind: How many times in my life have I missed incredible stories because I was too proud or afraid to be fully present? How many times am I so preoccupied with my agenda that I miss the stories of students, bus drivers, homeless people, volunteers, and everyone else who crosses my path each day? At that moment, the exchange of fans for friends became very real to me.

Barbara's interruption that day in the classroom jolted me out of my comfort zone, but being fully present still doesn't come naturally to me. It continues to be a struggle, but it's one I need to fight and win.

INVITING ENVY

In our world filled with social media, we need to be more social and use less media. I'm certainly not against all the advances of modern technology, but we need to step back and look at how they are affecting us—or at least, *I* need to evaluate how they are affecting *me*. As I have thought more about how social media is used, I realize it is often more about self-protection than meaningful connections. Personally, I positioned myself to project an identity as the competent leader or the cool friend. It's easy to fall into the trap of defining your identity to many people rather than being vulnerable with a chosen few. Sometime in my past I had concluded that if people know less of me, I have a better chance of impressing them. Vulnerability seemed risky, so I carefully avoided it.

> It's interesting that many psychologists say that one of the chief fears of humanity is being alone, but that fear exists in tension with another one: the fear of being fully known.

It's interesting that many psychologists say that one of the chief fears of humanity is being alone, but that fear exists in tension with another one: the fear of being fully known. On Facebook and Instagram, we present only those things we want people to know about us.

In an article about the dangers of posing online, Shauna Niequist warned people against "Instagram's Envy Effect." She noted that when people are online, they frequently tell partial truths and post pictures designed to impress. They show the picture-perfect dinner photo, but carefully avoid pictures of the mess that had to be cleaned up afterward. They share the photo of the happy couple on the mountain, but not the fight that happened an hour before. And think of all the toddler birthday bash pictures you've seen. How often do you see shots of the tantrum that occurred just moments later? Niequist explains:

> "My life looks better on the Internet than it does in real life. Everyone's life looks better on the Internet than it does in real life. The Internet is partial truths—we get to decide what people see and what they don't. That's why it's safer short term. And that's why it's much, much more dangerous long term. Because community—the rich kind, the transforming kind, the valuable and difficult kind—doesn't happen in partial truths and well-edited photo collections on Instagram. Community happens when we hear each other's actual voices, when we enter one another's actual homes, with actual messes, around actual tables telling stories that ramble on beyond 140 pithy characters."[6]

I understand the allure of creating an image. It looks more impressive to post a picture of a large group of people enjoying a terrific meal than one of a couple of close friends in a corner of a restaurant or around the kitchen table. The former produces celebrity status; the latter ignores status—and risks allowing others to think we're not cool and connected. One tries to capture the event for everyone to see; the other merely reflects genuine friendship. Real relationships aren't glamorous, but they are far more important than notoriety.

I was with a group of friends who met a popular singer before his concert. We all got pictures of the group posing with him, and for the next 15 minutes everybody tried to post a picture with the right filter and the right caption to the right people. During those 15 minutes, we missed a rare opportunity to connect with the singer!

It has become a common scene at restaurants and family dinner tables: people sit in silence while they email or text—sometimes to others at the same table! Being preoccupied with social media is also a sign of a classically bad first date. Rather than working through an awkward silence and starting a conversation, both parties sit and text the people who set them up to complain how horrible it's turning out.

We're sometimes called "the heads down generation" because we're so often on our phones. There is something very wrong about using our smart phones as our main communication tool. I have been guilty of it, but I'm determined to change.

The other feature that makes online posing so insidious is that we usually look at friends' posts when we're bored—at moments when we're especially vulnerable to deception and envy. If I'm doing something that has real meaning, I'm fully involved in it. The experience is filling my soul, so I'm not envying someone else's reality-altered half-truths with a sense of despair. One person's partial truths presented on social media contribute to someone else's unrealistic expectations, which can lead to genuine depression. In some cases social media is not just a minor distraction; it's a life-killing obsession.

The nature of modern communication consumes our attention and robs us of the ability to "be all there in the moment." Most of us are never far away from our phones. Even if we're not expecting a particular person to call, text, or email, we anticipate somebody will contact us at any moment. Linda Stone, formerly of Apple and Microsoft, coined the term "continuous partial attention" to describe the constant distractions of our communication devices. She writes:

> "To pay continuous partial attention is to pay partial attention—CONTINUOUSLY. It is motivated by a desire to be a LIVE node on the network. Another way of saying this is that we want to connect and be connected. We want to effectively scan for opportunity and optimize for the best opportunities, activities, and contacts, in any given moment. To be busy, to be connected, is to be alive, to be recognized, and to matter. We pay continuous partial attention in an effort NOT TO MISS ANYTHING. It is an always-on, anywhere, anytime, any place behavior that involves an artificial sense of constant crisis. We are always in high alert when we pay continuous partial attention. This artificial sense of constant crisis is more typical of continuous partial attention than it is of multi-tasking."[7]

If we're not careful, our hearts will stay tuned to our system of communication instead of the people themselves.

RISK AND REWARD

Please don't misunderstand me. I'm not suggesting that we bear our deepest sins, hurts, and desires to everybody we meet. We have to be realistic about the risk of vulnerability—especially in an increasingly superficial culture that instantly shares virtually everything. We need to pick our spots carefully, take small steps to see if trust has been established, and keep taking steps as the relationship deepens. This is a process, sometimes a long process, and one that is essential in our most important relationships with family and close friends.

The risks are very real. When we have the courage to share our hearts, we may receive criticism instead of support, quick answers instead of understanding and patience, or a cold shoulder instead of one to cry on.

But others take a risk when they talk to us, as well. When they share a long-buried fear or a cherished dream, are we listening . . . or thinking about our next appointment? Are we quick to reply with something we think will trump what they are saying? Do we offer simplistic solutions to life's deepest and most complex problems because we feel so uncomfortable with ambiguity and the process of grief and forgiveness?

> If we want others to be trusted friends, we need to be trustworthy, too—and it might be up to us to initiate the process.

Friendship is always a two-way street. If we want others to be trusted friends, we need to be trustworthy, too—and it might be up to us to initiate the process.

We find out who our real friends are when we go through emotional and spiritual valleys. During good times it's easy to think people are our friends because we laugh together, commiserate when our team loses, and celebrate when our cause succeeds. That level of relationship is fine as far as it goes, but we need more, and we need to give more. How many of those relationships endure when you get a dreaded diagnosis, an engagement falls apart, your career takes a nosedive, you're flat broke, or you've done something that produces oceans of shame? Your true friends will step forward in these critical moments (and not just to "fix" you). Similarly, you become a real friend when you uplift others who face similar calamities.

Who cares if you're "killing it on Facebook today"? Suffering people only care if you turn off your tablet, put your phone on silent, and look into their eyes with compassion and empathy. The problem, of course, is that if we want this level of relationship during the tough times, it first has to be cultivated during the good times so our connections are solid. If we don't choose to develop strong relationships when things are good, the bonds of friendship won't magically and suddenly appear when we need them.

We use both visible and invisible walls to protect ourselves. Two very evident walls are intimidation and isolation. We may try to scare people into submission by looking and sounding fierce, or we may take the opposite approach and avoid all meaningful contact by becoming noticeably absent. But we also build plenty of invisible walls. We engage in pleasant conversations, appearing confident and secure, but we use our smiles and witty banter to keep people from knowing what's really going on in our hearts. When others walk away, we hope they conclude we're sharp or nice or funny (preferably, all three), and we desperately hope they won't uncover what we're hiding.

We can have a dozen good reasons for keeping people away from us. At least, they may seem like very good reasons. Perhaps you have been hurt so badly in the past that you can't imagine letting anyone get close again. With every new interaction, you anticipate another betrayal, not understanding and support. Or you may have done something so bad in the past that you're terrified of someone finding out about it. Keeping it a secret is the logical strategy to avoid exposure and humiliation.

Or maybe you don't have deep dark secrets. Maybe you've just come to believe that you're such a loser that nobody would like you if they really knew you. Some people conclude that they are terribly dull and uninteresting, and they feel much more comfortable playing a role that projects a different image.

Real friendship is based on common interests, some of them surprisingly simple. Countless strong relationships have begun because two people were fans of the same team or shared a mutual interest in fashion or football or cooking. The simplest beginning, though, can blossom into much more.

C.S. Lewis explained the nature of friendship:

"Friendship arises out of mere Companionship when two or more of the companions discover that they have in common some insight or interest or even taste which the others do not share and which, till that moment, each believed to be his own unique treasure (or burden). The typical expression of opening Friendship would be something like, 'What? You too? I thought I was the only one.' . . . It is when two such persons discover one another, when, whether with immense difficulties and semi-articulate fumblings or with what would seem to us amazing and elliptical speed, they share their vision—it is then that Friendship is born. And instantly they stand together in an immense solitude."[8]

When we take a step to be a little vulnerable, it give others permission to take a step in return. There are no guarantees, but each step brings two people closer to greater understanding, kindness, and encouragement. Slowly, trust becomes a solid rock in the relationship, and a valuable bond is forged. This level of friendship has limits. You can't establish it with masses of people. It requires much time and energy. But it can happen with a few people, so choose wisely. When vulnerable friendships are formed, our lives are much richer than ever before.

That day in Cape Town, Barbara Dooley helped me see my need to exchange fans for friendship, but it's a calculation I have to make every day. I have to deny my compulsion to manage my image and trust that someone somewhere will love and accept me even if they know the truth about me. It's not that "the truth" is so horrible. I'm not an ax murderer, and I haven't embezzled billions from investors. But the truth is that I am thoroughly human, filled with a mixture of flaws, dreams, desires, discouragement, and hopes for the future. When I stop managing my image, I'm taking a big risk, but I'm also letting people get to know me. Those who look behind the mask and still care become better friends than I ever imagined. It's an exchange that has been hard, but it's one of the most valuable of my life.

MAKING THE CHANGE

Perhaps the hardest part of making this exchange is acknowledging the need to. Since humans first appeared on the planet, they have put up walls to protect themselves and manage their images, but our generation has become so distracted and consumed by social media that many don't even realize they have shallow relationships. When superficial connections are the only ones we've ever known, they seem completely normal. We think we have 1,000 friends because Facebook (or Twitter, Instagram, or Pinterest) says so. But those "friends" are virtual, not real. Too many of us are settling for counterfeit connections.

To make the exchange from fans to friends, I try to move my communications one notch forward. Instead of replying to a tweet, I send an email. In response to an email, I pick up the phone to call the person.

> Our values are reflected in our choices.

Instead of calling, I offer to meet for a cup of coffee. When I'm with people, I try to make a point of being fully present.

Our values are reflected in our choices. If I pay more attention to a buzzing phone than the person in front of me, I probably need to turn the phone off during conversations. Some experts recommend taking one day a week off from social media, or an hour a day, or some other period of time so we're not "always on." They call it "a technology fast." We need a plan to avoid letting social media dictate the quality of our relationships.

Bubba Watson went a big step further. Watson, a professional golfer, decided to skip the prestigious Players Championship in 2012 because he wanted to spend more time with his wife and adopted son. He explained in a tweet, "The Players is one of the best weeks of the year, but bonding with my son and wife is what it is all about right now." He later added, "Sorry to disappoint fans but the Players has one of the best fields all year, tourney is more than fine without me."[9] His withdrawal from the tournament set the Twitter world ablaze, but it wasn't a hard choice for him. He simply values his family and wanted to spend more time with them. Watson has listed his life's priorities as God, his family, his Dukes of Hazzard car, and golf—in that order.

My friend and mentor, Dr. Ike Reighard, says that when he was an elementary school safety patrol boy he was taught one simple lesson: stop, look, and listen. I've seen and heard a lot of messages about improving communication in business and other relationships, but I have yet to find any advice that is clearer, simpler, or better. No matter whom I'm with, I need to stop whatever I'm doing so I'm not distracted, focus my eyes and my heart on the person in front of me, and really listen to what is being said. I know I'm really listening if I ask follow-up questions. If I don't ask any, I have probably checked out, and I'm thinking about the next thing I want to do. When I practice stopping, looking, and listening, I build real connections with people. When I don't, I'm showing I don't really care that much about them. This simple principle worked for Dr. Reighard on the school crosswalk, and it works for me in every conversation.

But before you start a search for trustworthy people with whom you can share your life, you might want to consider the advice of Zig Ziglar. He has said, "If you go out looking for friends, you're going to find they are very scarce. If you go out to be a friend, you'll find them everywhere."

If you want authenticity, acceptance, and encouragement from a few trusted friends, you have to prove that *you* are authentic, accepting, and encouraging to others—especially when they are going through tough times.

And again, we can't take risk out of the equation. If you want complete control and protection from being hurt, you will never establish relationships that are meaningful. Relationships are always messy, and hurt people hurt people. The old movie tagline purported that in good relationships, "love means *never* having to say you're sorry." The opposite is actually true. In strong relationships, love means *often* saying you're sorry.

I'm not suggesting, though, that we use being wounded and pitiful as a foundation for relationships. It is just as wrong to project a deceptive image of weakness to elicit sympathy as it is to project a false image of strength to impress people. Both are image management, both are manipulative, and both erode trust and respect.

Life isn't like a computer program that offers predictable outcomes. When you move toward people and take a small risk to be open, you may be pleasantly surprised, or you may be disappointed. If the person doesn't treat you with respect, don't be crushed, and don't give up. Maintain your integrity, kindness, and honesty. Continue to treat people the way you want to be treated. Sooner or later you'll find a few really good friends—people who know the best and the worst about you and who love you all the same. A few people of that caliber are enough, and they will mean the world to you.

Great dramas involve a lot of conflicts, twists, and turns throughout the story. Resolution doesn't take place until the final scenes. Great relationships may also have a lot of conflict. Most of us assume conflict is the worst thing in the world. We live with the unrealistic, glowing expectations of an Instagram culture, so we think everything should be picture perfect. When we experience disappointments, disagreements, and real conflict, we're tempted to bail out long before the problem can resolve.

The problem at hand often has roots in a deeper, darker place: unresolved wounds of the past. We react to relatively minor events today because they trigger something long buried, rotten, and unresolved. Newlyweds or young singles who are dating are often startled at their partner's overreaction to a seemingly innocent comment or event, and they wonder, "What was *that* about?" To get to the source, we have to dig—and we may have to help others dig—into the fears and hurts of the past. The previous events of our lives make a big difference in our current responses. It may be painful to uncover and expose them, but it's essential if we're going to clear away the clutter and be free from the pain of the past.

Forgiveness is essential in any real relationship, but most of us aren't very good at it. We minimize the offense. ("It wasn't that bad.") We excuse the offender. ("Oh, she didn't really mean it.") We deny it happened at all. ("Lied to me? No, it never happened.") We try all these tactics to get past the awkward feelings as quickly as possible, but none of them work. They only shove the pain down into our hearts where it festers into resentment.

Author Lewis Smedes advocates ruthless honesty as a path to genuine forgiveness. He wrote, "When we forgive evil we do not excuse it, we do not tolerate it, we do not smother it. We look the evil full in the face, call it what it is, let its horror shock and stun and enrage us, and only then do we forgive it."[10]

Our capacity and motivation to forgive come out of our experience of being forgiven. If we have trouble forgiving those who hurt us, we need to experience forgiveness more fully so we can draw from a full well. If we think, *I would never treat anybody like he treated me,* we feel superior, and we believe we're completely justified in withholding forgiveness. When that happens we need to look in the mirror and see our own flaws. No, we may not have treated anyone in that specific way, but we have lied, betrayed, and cheated others. We are all deeply flawed people. If we don't detect any of those sins in our past, we may have another problem—an even bigger one: self-righteousness. Forgiving people isn't an add-on in relationships. It's essential because being close inevitably produces sparks. Forgiveness expresses, restores, and builds love between people.

Great friends aren't plastic and perfect. They make mistakes, as we do, but they are honest and kind. I am very grateful for friends who have learned to be skilled in the art of forgiveness, and I want to be that kind of friend.

In every gripping story, someone risks everything for another person. In every great relationship, someone has been willing to risk losing control, being hurt, and experiencing disappointment—and works to resolve those things so the relationship is stronger than ever. In the last few years I've gotten to do a lot of really cool things: cage diving with great white sharks, trekking around mountain gorillas, going on big game safaris, and traveling in the Greek isles. But my favorite memories are the times I spent with a friend or two when we were struggling with

a huge problem or laughing at
something one of us did. People always trump places.

> People always trump places.

A few people are masters at connecting with people. Betty Siegel is one of them. Dr. Siegel was the President of Kennesaw State University for over 25 years. Under her leadership, the school grew from 2000 to more than 20,000 students. Many administrators with her clout would wall themselves off from other people and have a comfortable leadership job while others handled the crowds, but she did just the opposite. She engaged people at all levels.

Most mornings Dr. Siegel had breakfast at the Waffle House near campus. Students loved her, and many would stop by her table to talk. Almost invariably, she asked them, "Who is a professor or someone else at our university who has made a difference in your life?" The students would think for a moment and then recall a professor, teacher's assistant, administrator, janitor, or someone else who had helped them. Dr. Siegel would write the person's name on the back of a napkin. Later she would find that individual, give him or her the napkin, and express her appreciation for that person's impact on a student's life. The person could then redeem the napkin for a free breakfast at Waffle House, compliments of Dr. Siegel. However, most of the napkin recipients never took her up on that free meal. Many professors and teachers cherished those napkins and held onto them. Some even got them framed, as a special honor she had given them.

Dr. Siegel is a wonderful example of how to build relationships in an organization, but you don't have to be the president of a large institution or the CEO of a big business to make a difference. People at every level can shape the culture of an organization, nonprofit, school, or club.

To overcome the distraction of social media and build real relationships—to exchange fans for friends—let me review what I have suggested:

- Wherever you are, be all there.
- Be aware of the inherent superficiality of social media. (And it doesn't look like it's going to change.)
- Fast an hour a day or a day a week (or both) from social media.
- Move your connectivity a notch forward: instead of texting or emailing, make a call; instead of calling, have coffee with the person.
- Don't try so hard to find a trustworthy friend. Be that friend instead.
- Adjust your expectations. Be realistic about the messiness of relationships, but realize they're worth the effort.
- Take steps of vulnerability, one at a time.
- Be selectively open. Don't share too much too soon, but be willing to take at least a small risk with the right people.
- Understand your story so you can see why you over- or under-react to particular people, stresses, or events.
- Develop the art and skill of being a good forgiver.
- Value people more than success.
- Stop, look, and listen to the people in front of you.
- Look for things to applaud in people's lives. Be rigorously thankful, supportive, and encouraging.

A few years ago Supreme Court Justice Clarence Thomas gave a compelling and unusual speech at a graduation. At most commencement ceremonies the speeches focus on the students' achievements and their futures. But Justice Thomas did the reverse. He told the crowd to remember that the reason they had gotten to this point in their lives was only because others had sacrificed for them. Then he told a story about his eighth grade teacher. Years after he left the school, he returned to his hometown and went to her room to express his gratitude for her profound impact on his life. He said that since she had taught more than 40 years, he assumed he was among a long list of students who had come back to thank her. She told him, "No, you're the first."

When that teacher was 95 years old, Justice Thomas went to visit her at a retirement center in New Jersey. In her small room that day, she pointed out the things that were to be given away upon her passing: a rosary, a prayer book, and some other items. Then she pointed to a picture of her with Justice Thomas that sat on her nightstand. She picked it up, and holding it she said, "This goes in my coffin with me."

Justice Thomas encouraged the students graduating that day to thank the people who had sacrificed to help them get to that pivotal point in their lives. Thanking people builds strong bonds, smoothes rough spots, and deepens understanding of what really matters.

I'm still very much in the process of exchanging fans for friends, but I'm learning. It's one of the most challenging and important choices I make every day. You may have a thousand superficial friends, but if you're like me, that's not enough. Developing great friendships is a process, and there are few simple answers. No matter how long it takes, don't give up. The ability to create meaningful friendships will have a powerful impact on every other relationship in your life: in your marriage, with your kids, in your career, and at your church.

> *"Friendship is unnecessary, like philosophy, like art. . . . It has no survival value; rather it is one of those things which give value to survival."*
> —C.S. Lewis

THINK ABOUT IT . . .

Before you read this chapter, how would you have described the impact of social media on relationships? Has this chapter changed your mind? If so, how?

What are some practical things you can do to lessen the impact of social media on you, and what can you do to build authentic relationships?

What difference would it make for you to be "all there" in conversations? How can you apply the principles of stop, look, and listen?

How can you be a better friend so you attract good friends?

Who do you need to thank for helping you get where you are today?

8

CHAPTER 3

EXCHANGING DOLLARS
FOR DIFFERENCE

"It's easy to make a buck. It's a lot tougher to make a difference."
—Tom Brokaw

*D*uring its first three years, our organization had grown. The four members of the original team had made significant sacrifices to get it up and running. We had invested our time and our hearts in this mission, although we had made very little money. At last the program was on solid financial footing, and we could finally expect to make a decent salary—not extravagant by any means, but enough to pay the bills each month. That was a big improvement!

From the beginning our goal had been to create environments that foster leadership and service. Our study abroad program was just one tool to reach that goal, and that model was working really well. But I felt there was a problem: our audience was too narrow. The vast majority of students who could afford to travel were from affluent backgrounds. I certainly valued our impact on that group, but I wanted to include more people. I wanted to engage, expose, and equip students—and for that matter, all individuals—across the socio-economic spectrum.

I realized there was at least one college student who could never have gone on one of our trips—me. My parents couldn't have afforded the steep price. I don't believe leadership should be limited to any class or group of people, so I began to explore other ways to accomplish our goals with a more diverse population of students.

Our team had always been open to other possibilities, so we began some very important conversations. I told them how I had envisioned a conference—not just any conference, but an inspiring, catalytic event that would propel students into greater effectiveness as young leaders. We could take a lot of the principles we used in study abroad trips and adapt them to a local setting that was accessible to all students.

As our team talked, a dividing line gradually became clear. It soon became obvious that the problem was that the conference didn't fit our existing business model. I kept trying to think of ways we could incorporate both models, but we realized that approach simply wasn't feasible.

After many long hours of discussions, my choice crystallized: I could remain a partner in the study abroad program, or I could leave to chase another dream. It wasn't easy to pick between two equally valid visions. I still believed in the study abroad program. I had brought my best contacts to the organization to teach and inspire students. I was still fully supportive of what we were doing, but my heart tugged me toward the vast, untapped group of students with amazing potential but limited resources.

I realized that if I stayed where I was, I would make an adequate income—for the first time in three years. If I left to follow the new vision, I would have to start over with new sacrifices of time, comfort, and money. In addition, I had just recruited 140 students for the next program. Chasing my new dream meant they would go without me . . . and I don't like feeling left out of anything!

It was one of the toughest decisions I've ever faced, but I knew what I needed to do. I wished my friends at the other organization well and left to launch a new venture. We called it ADDO, which means *inspire* in Latin. Our first conference, the ADDO Gathering, was held in Atlanta. It was a fantastic success in some ways, and a colossal failure in others. We attracted the broad spectrum of students I wanted to reach. Some came from elite private schools and parked their Range Rovers in the lot while others came from the inner city on school buses. For some, the only meal they ate that day was the free sandwich we served for lunch.

The conference content was terrific. The speakers had the perfect blend of challenge, inspiration, and practical application, but we didn't merely talk about the importance of serving. Before lunch we worked together to pack 25,000 meals to ship to hungry people in Haiti. When the students went home, we knew we had made a difference in their lives. The problem? We lost money. Just imagine: after all that planning and execution, the conference didn't break even. We had started at zero, and now we were in the hole!

Was it worth it? Two years later I was invited to speak at a local high school. Bella, the young lady who invited me, told me that she had been at our first ADDO Gathering. She said that after hearing one of the speakers she had been inspired to start a program for high school girls to mentor middle school girls through some of the toughest years of their lives. I asked who had invited her to come to the conference. She smiled and said, "Really, nobody. I read about it in the local newspaper." That had been enough to capture her interest. Bella was a leader with incredible potential. Our money-losing event had given her the gentle nudge she needed to do something remarkable, and now more than a third of the girls at her school are involved with and impacted by the program she started. So yes, I would say it was worth it.

The question in any business venture isn't whether or not to make money. I'm a full-fledged, card-carrying capitalist, and I believe it's important for every business to make a profit. But we need to order our priorities. If the goal is money, customers and clients become tools we manipulate. If, however, the goal is making a difference in people's lives—with inspiring events, great products, or effective services—dollars will flow where needs are being met. I'm not talking only about nonprofit organizations and mission-minded goals. Businesses that reveal needs and creatively meet them at a fair price sell a lot of products. The most successful companies are those that value their customers and have acute intuition about what's important to them. Then they create products and services to meet those needs.

> The most successful companies are those that value their customers and have acute intuition about what's important to them.

One of the main reasons I was willing to exchange dollars to make a difference was that I saw it modeled by my friend Garrett. He has never met a challenge he didn't like. I don't think he knows what the word "settle" means. He's always dreaming, pushing, and imagining new ways to make a difference. Garrett had started HERO for Children, UGA HEROs, and he was one of the co-founders in creating the new study abroad program. He was involved in all the conversations about staying or leaving. Ultimately, he was the one who started ADDO with me. He's my best friend and business partner. More than anyone I know, Garrett is willing to make exchanges.

Since I've known him, I've marveled at Garrett's courage to make big decisions. He was the youngest student body president in the history of the University of Georgia. He won the inaugural Courts Scholarship that allowed him to go anywhere in the world to work and study. He had never been out of the country, so he put one finger on Georgia on a globe and reached as far as he could to the other side. His other finger was on Hong Kong. He went there as an investment banking intern for Merrill Lynch. Out of their ten interns, nine were from prestigious Ivy League schools; Garrett was from a public school in the South.

He dove into his work, and he marveled at the intense dedication of everyone around him. Something, though, appeared terribly wrong. His boss missed an anniversary with his wife as well as his daughter's fourth birthday party. Garrett realized his boss's obsessive drive to succeed in business wasn't how he wanted his life to look in 10 or 20 years. No amount of money was worth that price. He took what he had earned and moved to Africa.

A lot of his professors and mentors thought he was nuts. He had landed a plum job with one of the best companies in the world. He was on track to make a six-figure salary right out of college, and the sky was the limit from there. But he sacrificed the tailored suits, the job in the corner office of the high rise in Hong Kong, and the promise of a position on Wall Street. He gave them up to go walk the slums of Kenya where he saw firsthand the devastation of HIV/AIDS on the children.

When Garrett came back to the university, he started a nonprofit organization that would help children affected by that disease in the United States. He drove an old, beat-up car, lived with his parents, and inspired thousands of students to get involved in caring for children who had previously been invisible to them.

If I hadn't seen Garrett make the exchange from dollars to difference several times already, I'm not sure I could have done it. And it didn't hurt that he was going to become my business partner in ADDO.

We certainly weren't naïve when we started ADDO. Garrett had even more experience than I did in starting new organizations, but we both fully understood the sacrifices we could expect in the first few years—if our new venture became successful at all. In an article for *Forbes Magazine*, Dave Feinleib observed that eight out of ten startup companies fail within the first three years.[11] All began with hope, enthusiasm, and a grand vision. None of them planned to fold, but it happens. Garrett and I fully understood this grim statistic, but we were willing to take the risk anyway.

During those years my mother would sometimes kid me about the craziness of our decision to risk monetary security for a chance to build leaders on a wider, deeper scale. She sometimes laughed and said, "I thought you were going to be rich and buy a beach house for your father and me!" No one could be more supportive than my parents, but she made a good point. It does seem a bit insane to attempt what we were hoping to do.

> In many ways, ADDO is designed to produce people just like our parents.

Actually, Garrett and I were starting ADDO because of people like his parents and mine. They aren't wealthy. They couldn't afford to study abroad when they were young, and they couldn't afford to pay for Garrett and me to travel the world. They are, however, quiet leaders who serve gladly and faithfully. In many ways, ADDO is designed to produce people just like our parents.

Ordering Priorities

There's nothing wrong with making money. Some people misquote the Bible and proclaim, "Money is the root of all evil." However, what is actually written is, "For *the love of* money is the root of all evil" (1 Timothy. 6:10, KJV, italics added). That's a big difference!

Having money opens new doors. It allows people to ask: "What is possible?" and "What pursuits are supremely valuable?" One of the most important tasks in life—and a task we need to do every day we're alive—is to put our priorities in order.

Many years ago Augustine said the problem with humanity is "disordered loves." He said there's nothing wrong with admiring beautiful bodies, enjoying delicious foods, and having fine homes, but those pursuits aren't as important as people. Our families and friends are much more significant than making more money so we can appear more successful.

But we are created for even more than enjoying good relationships. We are designed to love God and then love people as an overflow of our experience of God's kindness and compassion (Mark 12:28-31). We aren't truly fulfilled until we know our lives count.

Robert Kennedy understood the inherent value of sacrifice for a greater good. He said:

> "Few will have the greatness to bend history itself, but each of us can work to change a small portion of events. It is from numberless diverse acts of courage and belief that human history is shaped. Each time a man stands up for an ideal, or acts to improve the lot of others, or strikes out against injustice, he sends forth a tiny ripple of hope, and crossing each other from a million different centers of energy and daring those ripples build a current which can sweep down the mightiest walls of oppression and resistance."[12]

The cost of disordered priorities is high. When we choose dollars over making a difference, we're putting a higher priority on the things dollars can buy: nice stuff, fun times, comfort, exciting vacations, and especially, the prestige of having arrived. In this pursuit, we impoverish our souls, and we rob others of our investment in making their lives more fulfilling. Adrian Rogers warned, "Never let the things money can buy rob you of the things money can't buy."

Before we are willing to make this exchange, we need a counterintuitive view of life: we gain by losing, we become richer by giving away, we get power by serving, and we become stronger when we admit we're weak. When we're young, we tend to "keep score" by noting who has more nice stuff, but as we get older the scoring system changes—if we learn anything from watching people wreck their lives chasing dollars and possessions. Sooner or later we realize dollars only have significance if used to make a difference in the lives of others.

We can make two very different errors when it comes to making money a top priority. Some people value money for what it can buy. Quite often, such people are willing to go into debt to acquire enough stuff to impress others. They claim not to care much about money for its own sake, but they desperately want to have a nice car, beautiful clothes, the latest technology, cutting edge sports equipment, meals at great restaurants, and glamorous trips. These things, they're convinced, are essential for what they really crave—popularity and power. To them, money is a means to an end, but the end isn't making a *difference*; it's making an *impression*.

The other error is hoarding—refusing to spend money unless it's absolutely necessary, and even then, resenting every penny spent. People with this mentality are fewer, but they're out there. To them, money means security. Having enough would give them peace of mind, but they never have enough. They don't daydream about getting the latest fashions or going to exotic destinations with friends. They dream about making more money to fatten their savings accounts and portfolios, and they worry about not having all they need.

Both groups of people—spenders and hoarders—use money to gain a sense of security and significance. In that sense they are alike, but they use very different strategies.

A lot of my friends are turned off when attending churches that talk a lot about giving. If pastors are perpetually asking for money, people have good reason to be disturbed. But Jesus talked about money more than any other subject—more than eternity, more than relationships, and more than political power. Why was it so often the topic of his messages? Because the way we handle money reveals the deepest desires of our hearts. Our use of money and our attitudes toward it—either in using it to gain popularity and power, or hoarding it—demonstrate where we put our security. Valuing dollars over making a difference is entirely normal in human nature and in our culture.

One pastor commented that countless people have confessed the full range of sins to him . . . all except one. He says no one has ever confessed the sin of greed because everyone thinks his view of money is completely normal. Jesus and every other great leader know that money can't give us the one thing we all desperately need—purpose. That has to come from a different source. When we have a vision for our lives and a reason to get up each morning, money becomes a tool to make a difference in others' lives.

Obviously the exchange has to happen on a personal level, but as I have said, corporations and nonprofits of every size also need to make the exchange. Their health and survival depend on proper priorities. If they put dollars first, they often make choices that disregard the needs of the people they claim to serve. But if they put people's needs first, they will create goods and services that really matter, and they will grow.

My very first job was with Brookstone, a retail store that sells high-end products for homes and offices. One of the company slogans was, "We make things that make life better, easier, and more fun." I enjoyed working for a company that identified needs and provided quality products to meet those needs. Every day, the company delivered on its slogan's promise. When companies add value to people's lives, they will almost certainly make money. It's a sound business principle.

One of the biggest hindrances to making a difference is debt. The debtor is the slave of the lender, and quite literally, many people don't have the freedom to dive into activities

> When companies add value to people's lives, they will almost certainly make money.

that make a difference in the lives of others. Those who suffer under this burden have to devote their time and energy to meet the responsibilities of mortgages, loans, and other obligations. They become overextended, and they spend valuable energy worrying about making the next payment. People with too much debt aren't free to go to Africa to work with kids who have AIDS or to leave a steady job to become a lesser-paid teacher. They can't volunteer for neighborhood projects because they have to work overtime to make extra money. They can't coach a kids' baseball team because they are working two jobs.

As important as it is to have a plan to get out of debt, even more essential is to first craft a vision for your life. If you're convinced your life is going somewhere important, you'll be motivated to make better decisions about money. Instead of having disordered loves, you will rework your priorities. Money will then become a tool to reach far bigger goals than impressing friends or adding to your savings account. With a new vision for your life, you'll have a reason—a compelling reason—to make different choices about money.

My advice for people of my generation is to live frugally and give generously. Establish a lifestyle that enables you to be flexible and participate in things that capture your heart. You can always buy more stuff later, but starting well will serve you for the rest of your life. My advice for those who are up to their eyeballs in debt is to do everything possible to get out from under that heavy load. Lower your spending, pay off loans, and become free to respond to opportunities that come your way.[13]

MORE THAN MONEY

This chapter isn't really about money at all. It's about purpose and priorities. Plenty of books are available about how to make more money and/or get out of debt. They can be valuable, but only when we care about something more than money.

Even if you're in debt over your head, don't let the heavy pressure of making payments keep you from getting involved in caring for others. You pass people every day who are less fortunate or whose lives have been shattered by some kind of calamity. Stop and notice them, even if it's during your lunchtime. You may feel overwhelmed with all of your responsibilities, but many of those people would love to swap places with you. Open your eyes. See them. Start a dialogue and find out how you can help—even if it's only to lend a listening ear and a caring heart.

If you're in debt or just starting out in your career, you may not have many dollars to invest in causes, but you can give time and love. Volunteer at a homeless shelter, a food bank, or a nursing home. Grab a hammer and show up on a Saturday to build a house for Habitat for Humanity. Try it for one day. If it touches your heart, do it again when you can. Be generous with what you have—no matter what it is, or how little.

Bob Pierce is the founder of World Vision, an organization that cares for desperate needs, mostly in third-world countries. On his first trip overseas, he encountered a sick child. He suddenly felt overwhelmed with compassion. He prayed, "Let my heart be broken by the things that break the heart of God."[14]

The very last thing most people want is for their hearts to be broken. They want a comfortable, easy life—and protection from being exposed to poverty, disease, and death. If we want to make a difference, our hearts have to be shattered by the needs of others—whether they live on the other side of the globe or in the next bedroom. Only then will we do the hard work necessary to reorient our priorities. A disturbed heart is exceedingly uncomfortable, but it's the essential, driving force for this exchange.

> A disturbed heart is exceedingly uncomfortable, but it's the essential, driving force for this exchange.

When we make the exchange, we pay a price. I've had the opportunity to visit New York City and stay at a friend's penthouse and someone else's fancy summer vacation home at the beach. Those were spectacular places to stay, but then I get on the plane and come home to a different reality. Envy thrives on comparison, and this comparison is pretty stark! It would be easy to become jealous of my friends' lifestyles.

But some of my richest friends have told me they wish they were doing what I'm doing with ADDO. I'm not suggesting that what I'm doing is noble or that those who make a lot of money are shallow and phony. What I'm saying is that people have to find and follow their dreams, and if I weren't following mine I wouldn't be fulfilled.

Money alone isn't enough to capture our hearts. I would much rather have the passion to leverage every resource to change lives than to be solely devoted to making more money. This choice, as always, comes at a cost. I have to be willing to see it, face it, and keep choosing purpose over the perks dollars can buy.

The size and scope of a person's dream isn't the issue either. We can care deeply about something immediate and local—like being a loving and attentive parent to our kids—and make the exchange in order to improve their lives. Adrian Rogers commented, "It's about time we stopped spending money we don't have, to buy stuff we don't need, to impress people we don't like."

Even multi-national companies can change their priorities when a need breaks the hearts of the executives. For hundreds of years a condition called "river blindness" affected people in rural communities in Africa, the Middle East, and Latin America. In 1987, the pharmaceutical giant Merck stumbled upon a cure, but the accountants couldn't find a way for the new drug to make a profit for the company.

Instead of focusing solely on the dollars involved and turning their backs on those who were suffering, Merck executives created a public-private partnership to donate the drug to infected people. Today, more than a billion treatments for river blindness have helped 117,000 people in 28 countries. In several areas the disease was completely eradicated.

The program was so successful that new drug donation programs were implemented to help people who suffer from other diseases. Merck Chairman, President and CEO Kenneth C. Frazier commented, "We are humbled by the great work of the alliance of partners to protect future generations from a disease that carries devastating implications for people, families, healthcare systems and local economies."[15]

Let me make a few suggestions to encourage you to exchange dollars for making a difference:

- Be willing to be disturbed.
- Notice how much you're protecting your heart from seeing— and feeling the pain of—others' hurts.
- Be honest: Are you spending money to impress people? Are you hoarding it to feel more secure?
- Be generous with what you have . . . whatever resources of time, love, and money you possess.
- Spend time with people who have already made this exchange. Ask plenty of questions, and listen well.
- In businesses and organizations, focus on meeting needs instead of maximizing profits.
- If you're tempted to buy things on credit, think again.
- Buy what you can afford, not everything you want. Use cash whenever possible.
- Examine your motives for how you use money. Be honest if your real motivation is to impress people or to ensure your security.
- If you're in debt, take steps to get out. It's never too late to start. Small steps eventually add up so you can be free.

- Be aware that if you make this exchange, some people will think you're nuts, and others will admire your courage.
- If you want to make a bigger impact, focus more on the outcomes than your income. Dollars flow to where needs are being met.

Our lives are on a trajectory. The choices we make each day are, to a great extent, shaped by the choices we have already made. But we don't have to keep living with disordered priorities. We can change the trajectory.

To make the exchange from making dollars to making a difference, we need clarity and courage. A few years ago, I faced the very real choice between a comfortable salary and stable role . . . or the sacrifice of having very little money but following my heart. We face similar choices every day, but we recognize very few of them. I hope the stories and examples in this chapter have helped you identify at least one or two. Don't settle for the broken dream of using money to acquire more stuff. Follow your dream, and use money to fulfill it.

> *"Never forget that you are one of a kind. Never forget that if there weren't any need for you in all your uniqueness to be on this earth, you wouldn't be here in the first place. And never forget, no matter how overwhelming life's challenges and problems seem to be, that one person can make a difference in the world. In fact, it is always because of one person that all the changes that matter in the world come about. So be that one person."*
> —*Richard Buckminster Fuller*

THINK ABOUT IT . . .

Why is it so tempting to use money to impress people? What is the allure of hoarding money? Have you used either of these strategies? If so, what have been the results?

What are some signs a person has disordered priorities? What are the consequences?

To what extent are you free from debt so you can follow your dreams? What new options would you have if you were truly free from the burden of debt?

Which of the suggestions will you do first? What do you expect to happen?

8

CHAPTER 4

EXCHANGING EXPEDIENCE FOR EXCELLENCE

"It takes less time to do things right than to explain why you did it wrong."
—Henry Wadsworth Longfellow

I'm obsessed with completion. I want to accomplish a task, check off the box, and move on to the next goal. Most of the time my compulsion to finish projects is a strength. Sometimes, though, I cut corners that shouldn't be cut. My problem isn't that I try to find the *easy* way out; too often, problems arise because I settle for the *quickest* way to get things done.

Like most people, I invest time and abilities in the things that matter to me. If I care about a task, I take all the time needed to do it right. The problem is that I don't care about too many things, so I pursue excellence very selectively. To some degree, this is true for everybody. We can't be perfectionists about everything, or we would drive people (including ourselves) crazy! Some things, though, deserve more attention than I give them. So the question becomes: what is so important that it demands every ounce of energy and excellence I can pour into it, and which things don't need my very best?

TWO EXTREMES, SAME CAUSE

The exchange from expedience to excellence, like all the other exchanges, requires more than a superficial glance to see what's going on under the surface. Some people are completely comfortable with loose ends. They live, and even thrive, in ambiguity. Philosophers think deeply about the complexities of life and we respect their efforts even when they don't have all the details worked out. But many people avoid decisions and tolerate ambiguity simply because they're afraid to fail. Not completing tasks for fear of failure is the cousin of being obsessed with checking off boxes. Both attitudes are driven by an underlying fear, though the fear produces opposite behaviors.

Fear can cloud our thinking and limit our vision. If my compulsion to finish tasks is driven by fear, everything seems equally important. In fact, the only thing that's really important is the box with the check in it. But when I have more perception about my innate fear and the behavior it spawns, I can make better choices.

I have learned to see my responsibilities in three distinct tiers: (1) the things that really matter and need all of my creativity and energy; (2) the things that are important but not vital; and (3) the tasks that really aren't very important at all. If I can identify the category where a task belongs, I've gone a long way in determining when cutting corners is appropriate.

We need to avoid the two extremes: perfectionism and pervasive expedience. Perfectionism values good things too highly, but expedience doesn't value the most important things highly enough. In their own ways, both are behaviors of control freaks. Psychologist Les Parrott describes the mindset of a controlling perfectionist as "a 'will to conquer,' an 'instinct to master,' a 'manipulative drive,' a 'striving for superiority,' and an 'urge toward competence.' It doesn't really matter what you call it; if you've ever been repeatedly roped into someone else's ways of doing and being, you know what it feels like to be had by a Control Freak."[16]

Perfectionists live in a state of perpetual dissatisfaction. Even when they complete a project, they are never completely satisfied because it can't measure up to their exacting standards. But expedience for the sake of speed isn't any better, and certainly isn't a virtue. In fact, it's based on misplaced priorities. When I cut corners, I'm making a value judgment that something else (such as my time) is more valuable than the task or the people the task serves. Expedience isn't evil, wrong, or harmful, but expedience *at the cost of excellence in the things that matter* deadens our souls instead of enflaming them with renewed purpose.

Perfectionists and those who are compelled to speedily check off boxes are inherently insecure. They can't afford for anyone to see them fail. One covers up this insecurity by doing things with exquisite precision and patience; the other covers it up by getting it done quickly to show progress.

On both extremes, the results are a reflection of a person's identity. The perfectionist is determined to display only the very best, but often fails to get something worthwhile actually finished. The expedient person wants to show that she's effective and meets deadlines, but she sometimes puts her name on things that are less than her best.

WHO DO WE REPRESENT?

One of the best ways to cut through the deeply buried motivations toward perfectionism or expedience is to realize we're representing something bigger. Those of the Christian faith think of Paul's encouragement to "do all to the glory of God" (1 Corinthians 10:31). If we work with this higher goal in mind, it will drive us to pursue excellence in a healthy, positive way. The knowledge that we represent God should make a difference.

We also represent our families. In traditional cultures, the family name means everything. A person's actions can be a source of pride or shame for generations. Even in our land of opportunity and fresh starts where people are generally judged on their own merits, one's behavior still colors what people think about his or her family—parents, siblings, and children. Whether we realize it or not, we represent more than ourselves in every word and action.

WORTHY

It's easy to get out of balance. When priorities are driven by insecurity, we can become perfectionists who can't make decisions, control freaks who attempt to dominate and manipulate every situation, or box-checkers who value expedience more than people and causes. As always, clarity of purpose is essential. If our purpose remains distant and vague, it won't shape how we spend each day. If purpose doesn't make a difference in our choices all day every day, it's meaningless, because the way we spend each day determines the impact of our lives.

Many people drift from one activity to another or spend countless hours devoted to meaningless activities because nothing really matters to them. We need to find a pursuit that is worthy of excellence, a driving goal that elicits our

> When we identify a clearly defined purpose that's much bigger than our comfort and popularity, we have a reason to pursue excellence.

most creative thoughts and our most passionate activities. When we identify a clearly defined purpose that's much bigger than our comfort and popularity, we have a reason to pursue excellence. At that point, though, we face the very real tension of the choice between expedience and excellence.

It is not always easy to identify something worthy of our time and energy. Some of the biggest problems are the unrealistic expectations created by the media. I enjoy looking at travel magazines. The photos are spectacular, and I love to read the descriptions of vacation spots around the world. But I've been to some of those places, and I know that the photos and descriptions don't tell the whole story. The people who create those articles have an amazing talent to show the perfect sunset at the perfect beach with the perfect couple standing on the golden sand. If the photographer had used the wide-angle lens rather than the zoom, you might see the rest of the picture: the stinking dumpster near the hotel, the dead fish on the beach, and the long lines of traffic on the road to the resort.

In the same way, we need to take a step back and get an honest view of our lives and our situations. When we see charmed lives on Facebook and Instagram, we must remember those are poses. We live in a fallen world with imperfect people. Our expectations need to be ruthlessly realistic as well as rigorously optimistic. Optimism without realism can't stand the test of disappointment. When our high hopes are dashed, we will bail and miss out on some wonderful things because we insisted on perfect things.

One reason for unrealistic expectations is failing to understand that there are seasons in life. In certain seasons we may need to be devoted to become excellent students, parents, or employees. You might have a desire to move to Bali to work with natives, but if you have two young children, they need you at home right now . . . for another long while. You may get tired of reading to them every night, but you need to realize that every silly story is creating a bond that will last a lifetime.

You may feel unfulfilled working as an intern because you want to start your own business, but you need to understand that you're learning vital skills and internalizing important experiences. New opportunities will arise someday, but right now your present pursuits are worthy of your best energy and efforts.

At home and at work, we need to remind ourselves of the three tiers of priorities. If we put too much in the top category, we will quickly feel overwhelmed. We will be perfectionists about too many things, and we will neglect some very important things. But if we drift through life without putting *anything* on the "most important" list, everything will seem equally bland, no one will be pleased with us, and we will resent all the expectations and demands.

The pressures of a family and a career are enormous. We can't afford to consider a spouse and kids just another item to check off our list each day. They know if they matter to us, and the way we treat them now will shape them for the rest of their lives. We can't be perfect parents or perfect employees, but if we prioritize carefully and intelligently we will know we're investing our best in the people and tasks that matter most. Then we will be able to live with second best in the other areas.

There are no simple answers—no "one size fits all." But that's not an excuse for living on either end of the perfectionism-expedience continuum. My friends with children tell me that one thought colors their thinking: they will never have this time with their kids again. There are no do-overs. No matter what it takes, they want to be fully present in their children's lives. Even so, this clear principle sometimes requires flexibility. Times will come when a parent may need to invest additional time at work. The kids' future won't be imperiled as long as the increased work schedule is relatively brief and the family times remain rich and meaningful. But parents must resist becoming so involved in the new, demanding work schedule that it comes permanent, causing them to miss too much of their children's formative years.

Reorienting priorities is a constant struggle. The requirements and demands of our jobs change, the needs of our families shift as kids grow up, aging parents begin to need our help, and other factors can consume our time, attention, and energies. It's wise to zoom out regularly to look at where we're going, where we've been, and where we are right now. Otherwise we can easily suffer from the career and family forms of "mission creep," where we keep taking on more responsibilities until we're exhausted, resentful, and discouraged. We can lie to ourselves and our families by promising things will get better even though we're not making necessary changes. Eventually spouses, kids, and even our best friends no longer believe us, and we even lose faith in ourselves.

In their song, "American Dream," Casting Crowns describes the emptiness of misplaced priorities:

Well this American Dream is beginning to seem

More and more like a nightmare with every passing day.

"Daddy, can you come to my game?"

"Oh Baby, please don't work late."

Another wasted weekend and they are slipping away

'Cause he works all day and lies awake at night.

He tells them things are getting better

Just take a little more time.[17]

Students in college and grad school often are so invested in their future that they miss the present. They make expedient choices today and intend to pursue excellence later—when they graduate, enter their careers, or get married. But most students would benefit from a commitment to excellence while still on campus. It's not just that they need to learn from the courses they're taking. They also are developing habits for a lifetime. Perfectionists need to learn to loosen up a bit; those who are too expedient and unfocused need to screw the lid on a little tighter. They're representing their families in the classroom, and they're setting a pattern of priorities for their own futures.

But again, the same course of action may not be best for everyone. When I was a student, the process of setting priorities didn't lead to academic excellence. I was involved in many different activities, but helping kids affected by HIV/AIDS became the driving force in my life. It wasn't an academic pursuit, but it galvanized my purpose in life. I found what was important to me, and I wouldn't trade it for better grades. Yet when some of my friends clarified their priorities, they devoted more time to excellence in school. I exchanged expedience for excellence in a cause; they exchanged expedience for excellence in the classroom.

> All of us, though, need to keep zooming in and out until we find something worthy of every ounce of creativity and energy in us.

People may have similar hopes and dreams, but the path to fulfill those dreams may take them in very different directions. All of us, though, need to keep zooming in and out until we find something worthy of every ounce of creativity and energy in us.

HIGH SCHOOLS AND HELICOPTERS

My current organization, ADDO, has developed a relationship with Chick-fil-A to inspire and impact high school students. We have big plans to be in 1200 high schools in 20 states in the next few years. I am motivated by growth and change, and I don't want anything to slow me down!

After about three months of developing our strategy and curriculum, we conducted a beta test of our model. It went pretty well, but there were plenty of rough edges. As we analyzed the results, we met with David Salyers, the Vice President of National Marketing for Chick-fil-A. David wanted to make a point, but he made it the same way Jesus often did—he told us a story. He said that in the '90s, Chick-fil-A faced a big challenge. Another restaurant chain, Boston Market (Boston

Chicken at the time), was serving really good chicken and offered an excellent customer experience. Boston Market had a very aggressive growth strategy that threatened to cut into Chick-fil-A's market share.

The founder of Chick-fil-A, Truett Cathy, was called into a meeting with his top executives to discuss the dilemma. Plans were presented to accelerate growth and compete more effectively. Some of the strategies involved taking on debt and securing outside investors in order to grow more quickly. Cathy sat quietly during the long deliberations. Finally, he had heard enough. He pounded his fist on the table, which got everyone's attention because he's not a demonstrative man. When every eye was fixed on him, he said plainly, "We don't need to worry about getting *bigger*. We need to worry about getting *better*." Cathy paused for a second, and then he explained, "When we get better, our customers will demand that we get bigger."

That ended the conversation. Expedience wasn't the solution; excellence was. By the year 2000, Boston Market had filed for bankruptcy, while Chick-fil-A hit $1 billion in annual revenue. The commitment to excellence has served the company well. They now have over $4 billion in annual revenues. Truett Cathy didn't think growth was unimportant, but he realized that getting better was the key to sustainable growth.

A commitment to excellence doesn't eliminate risk. Sometimes it actually multiplies the risks we take. When I got involved with UGA HEROs, I led our fundraising effort. The most we had ever raised was $75,000 in one year, but I wanted to bring in far more. When I met with our faculty advisor, I told her that my goal was $300,000. She said, "Well, that's nice, but it won't happen. Why don't you be more realistic? How about a 33 percent increase? That would be $100,000."

We debated for a while, but I didn't want to back down from my goal because it wasn't an arbitrary number. Another organization on campus was bigger and better funded, and it had more students involved. Dance Marathon, which benefitted the Children's Miracle Network, had raised over $300,000 the year before. I wanted to match their level even though I was aware we had a long way to go to reach that goal.

Our student organizations raised money by having a kickoff event to enlist students as fundraisers—the more students at the kickoff, the more fundraisers would be asking friends and family for donations. Dance Marathon had invited the reigning Miss America to speak at their launch event. We invited Mark Richt. Coach Richt is a great guy, but no one would come out to hear him the way they would show up to see Miss America. We had to think of something—something really big to grab the headlines and get students involved in our kickoff.

Our organization was going to have an impact on 500 children that year, so we wanted to find a way to emphasize the number 500. We talked to our friends at Chick-fil-A and Coach Richt, and we created a promising strategy. Someone loaned us a cherry red helicopter, and Chick-fil-A donated 500 small stuffed cows with parachutes to drop from the sky. Each cow had a sticker that read: "UGA HEROs," "Coach Mark Richt," and the date and time for the event.

To get people to assemble where the drop would take place, we handed out thousands of invitations with the time and location. They were like the sign in *V for Vendetta*—they read, "Remember . . . Remember the 6th of September. Tate Plaza. 12:20 P.M." It was a guerilla marketing plan to arouse curiosity so students would come to see . . . something. They had no idea what to expect, but the buzz was building.

We got permission from the FAA to land the helicopter and then fly over campus. We got permission from Coach Richt to land the helicopter on his practice field and load the cows. We had everything ready to drop the cows at 12:20 at Tate Plaza on that Friday during lunch.

We had every detail lined up and secured . . . well, all but one. We hadn't gotten approval from the Campus Police. About 40 minutes before the drop, I got a call from Jimmy Williamson, the Campus Police Chief. He said in a gruff voice, "I heard you're planning to drop something out of a helicopter over my campus."

I answered, "Yes, sir. We have permission from the . . ."

"You don't have permission from me," he interrupted. "And it's not going to happen!"

I tried to explain that our whole fundraising strategy was based on getting students to our kickoff event, and we needed this dramatic cow drop to get their attention. If students didn't join us, I explained, they wouldn't raise money, and we wouldn't be able to help children throughout Georgia.

He was not impressed with my logic or zeal.

This was where risk raised its head. Garrett, the founder of the organization and my partner in crime, went with me to see Police Chief Williamson. We had to make this happen, and fast. After the chief explained his position again, Garrett asked, "What would happen if we pretend we didn't have this conversation and the drop happened as we planned?"

The police chief was furious! He barked, "That's not the right question, young man. I'll throw both of your butts in jail. That's what will happen!"

He turned to me and growled, "If you do this, young man, you won't graduate from this university."

I told him, "Sir, I'm supposed to speak at graduation."

His eyes flared and he snapped, "You won't have to worry about that!"

The helicopter was loaded with 500 little cows. It was warmed up and ready to go. Two of our students were in it, ready to throw the cows out. The pilot was waiting for word to take off. A thousand students were walking toward Tate Plaza. It was now or never, but I couldn't risk getting arrested and being thrown out of school just before I graduated.

Garrett, on the other hand, wasn't intimidated at all. When we walked outside, he whispered, "Kevin, if we get arrested, we'll be in all the headlines. Coach Richt will come to the jail to bail us out, and we'll be on Oprah next week. It'll be the best publicity we could possibly get!"

> Thankfully, I'm not writing this from a prison cell.

That's not exactly what I was thinking. My thoughts were, *I'll be arrested. I'll get kicked out of school. My parents will kill me.*

Thankfully, I'm not writing this from a prison cell. It didn't come to that. Five minutes before the designated drop, Chief Williamson changed his mind. He gave us an exception and let us toss little cows out of the helicopter. Tate Plaza was covered with students who were curious about what would happen at 12:20. When the helicopter flew over and the cows flew out, the parachutes took them all over the area. Some were still stuck in trees three years later. It was a glorious moment for UGA HEROs, but it was just the first piece of the fundraising puzzle.

When Coach Richt spoke a week later, we were amazed at the number of students who showed up. They signed up to raise money for children in Georgia affected with HIV/AIDS, and they got busy talking to people about our cause. Previously UGA HEROs had about 750 students involved; now over 2000 joined us.

The students spent a couple of months raising money. On December 1, World AIDS Day, we had a rally on the football field of a local high school where we played games in a HERO Olympics. It was a huge field day of fun for our students and children from around the state. At the end, we planned to reveal how much we had raised. The moment of high drama came when we positioned eight students in front of the crowd with big cards turned backwards. One by one, starting from the right, they turned their cards around to show the number. The first two were for the cents. Then dollars, tens of dollars, hundreds, thousands, and tens of thousands. One card remained. The last student turned it over to reveal a 3. We had raised $306,144.28 for children affected by HIV/AIDS! What a thrill! We became the one of the biggest charities on a college campus in the Southeast.

At every point in this drama, we could have settled for expedience instead of excellence. We could have settled for $100,000 as our goal, we could have done only a little more marketing than the previous year, and we could have just passed out fliers instead of dropping cows at Tate Plaza. But we wanted to do something special for the kids in Georgia. I'm glad we did. Thousands of people were involved in something they will always remember, and we helped more children than ever before. It just doesn't get any better than that.

Setting priorities and living by them is seldom as dramatic as the cow drop on a sunny afternoon at the University of Georgia, but it's always important.

> If chasing your dreams doesn't stretch you, your dreams aren't big enough.

Let's recap some of the elements of this exchange:

- Identify your tendencies to be a perfectionist or to cut too many corners and check off boxes.
- Understand the "control freak" drive.
- List your responsibilities in three categories: (1) those that require the dedication and discipline of excellence; (2) those that need considerable attention but not your best effort; and (3) those that aren't very important.
- If chasing your dreams doesn't stretch you, your dreams aren't big enough.
- In businesses and organizations, focus on getting better instead of getting bigger.
- Regularly zoom out to get the big picture of your priorities.
- In every role (friend, employee, employer, spouse, parent, etc.), consider whom you represent.
- Learn to live with some level of ambiguity, and focus on the things that are most important.

- Decide what you want and what you're willing to exchange for it. Establish your priorities, and go to work!
- Evaluate the risk of doing things with excellence. Is it worth it?

It takes experience, time, and some honest feedback to see clearly your position on the continuum between perfectionism and cutting corners for the sake of expedience. The exchange, though, won't happen until you see a bigger picture of your life. Identify the things that really matter, and don't let anything get in the way of your devotion to them. You can't do everything with excellence, but you can do a few things very well. Do those.

"Doing more things faster is no substitute for doing the right things."
—*Stephen Covey*

THINK ABOUT IT . . .

Where are you on the spectrum from perfectionism to cutting corners? Are you satisfied with where you are? Explain your answer.

List your most pressing responsibilities. Then separate them into the three categories: vital, important but not vital, and not very important.

What are some of the risks of being dedicated to excellence in at least one or two areas of your life? What are some risks of expedience?

In your current situation, what does it mean to "live with a measure of ambiguity"? How well are you managing that balance?

CHAPTER 5

EXCHANGING SHIFTING SANDS FOR SOLID ROCK

"Character cannot be developed in ease and quiet. Only through experience of trial and suffering can the soul be strengthened, ambition inspired, and success achieved."
—Helen Keller

*I*n the good times, we can coast along and enjoy the ride. Inevitably, though, we encounter extended periods of heartache or crushing moments that threaten us to the core. When pleasant experiences, warm relationships, and financial stability are taken away, what's left to stand on?

In the incredibly wealthy United States of America, it's easy to think that life should always be fun, easy, pleasant, and successful. That's the American dream, and people are living it every day. We *should* enjoy the good things in life, but it's dangerous to expect them to be permanent. Sooner or later, the hammer falls. Those who expect their lives to be consistently rosy are often blindsided by difficulties. They are confused and angry, and they don't know how to respond.

My friend Ike Reighard says, "Life is tissue-paper thin." He ought to know. Years ago, he and his wife Cindy were expecting the birth of their first child. Together in the delivery room, they anticipated the highest joy, but both the mother and child died in childbirth. That night Ike went home to an empty house, to a room perfectly decorated for their baby, and to a bed where he was completely alone. I'll tell you more about Ike later in this chapter.

It doesn't take an untimely death to devastate us. Any number of problems can shatter high hopes, cherished dreams, and lofty expectations. We can be floored by layoffs at work, being passed over for a promotion, the end of a marriage or other strong relationship, betrayal by a friend, a child with a disability, the discovery of a family member's longstanding secret addiction, a parent diagnosed with cancer, a best friend who takes a job in another state, a sibling deployed to a war zone, debilitating depression, chronic loneliness, years of grief due to unresolved hurts, and countless other painful scenarios.

When I speak about this topic, I see most eyes either light up or fill with tears. A few young people, though, look bored. Those are the ones who haven't been shaken yet, and they can't relate to what I'm saying. Tragedy hasn't invaded their lives, but someday they will hit rock bottom. It's guaranteed . . . a part of life.

When I travel to third-world countries, people seem to have more realistic expectations. In Cuba, Uganda, Indonesia, and many other parts of the world, people live every day surrounded by disease, death, destruction, disaster, and other heartaches. They aren't surprised when they suffer. They have learned that suffering is as much a part of life as comfort and conveniences—and in some countries, far more common.

In our culture, one of the most common reactions to calamity is to shake our fists at heaven and ask, "God, why did you let this happen?" The question reveals a deeply rooted sense of entitlement . . . the presumption that if God loves us, he surely wouldn't allow us to experience pain and loss.

Psychologist Larry Crabb observed that many people treat God as a "specially attentive waiter." When he gives us good service, we give him a tip of praise or a few dollars. When we don't get what we wanted, we complain to the management.[18]

If we don't expect heartaches, we certainly won't be prepared for them. Consequently, we overreact. We blame ourselves for being so stupid, we blame others for failing, and we blame God for not protecting us. Every disappointment is interpreted as a threat to our stability. The real problem, then, isn't the calamity itself; it's an incorrect perception of God as we experience the calamity.

Danny has been one of my best friends since kindergarten. When we were kids, we were inseparable. When he was about 12, he and his father went on a fishing trip. As they drove to their favorite lake, a drunk driver swerved in front of them. Danny's dad was killed in the collision. As an only child, Danny depended more than ever on his mother for love and support. When Danny was 23, his mother wasn't feeling well and tests revealed she had ALS (Lou Gehrig's Disease). Some people live many years with this debilitating deterioration of muscles, but Danny's mother died not long after her diagnosis. Danny found himself completely alone.

Danny refused to collapse into self-pity and resentment. He continued to move forward with life. A few years later he fell in love and asked a beautiful young woman to marry him. I was honored that he asked me to be his best man.

The week before the wedding I was winding down a month-long trip through Singapore, Australia, New Zealand, and Indonesia. I flew back early to be at the wedding. After the rehearsal dinner, Danny and I went to his hotel room to catch up. Throughout the conversation I wanted to ask him a question. I know that a girl dreams of a perfect wedding day as her father walks her down the aisle. Guys often have a brother standing beside them and parents sitting on the front row. Danny didn't have parents or siblings who would be at his wedding. I reflected back on the painful losses he had suffered and I asked, "Danny, how did you manage all that? How did you get from there to here?"

He smiled and replied, "Kevin, I realized that all I had was God, but he's all I need."

I had been living a dream. I presumed Danny had been living a nightmare, but he didn't see it that way at all. He found peace, hope, and love in something—actually, in Someone—far deeper than pleasant circumstances. Ike and Danny were very honest about the hurt and anger they experienced, but they didn't give up on God. Eventually, they found wisdom—not simple answers, but a deeper faith in the One who is ultimately wise. Ike often quotes the brilliant English pastor Charles Spurgeon:

"God is too good to be unkind.

He is too wise to be confused.

If I cannot trace His hand,

I can always trust His heart."

Faith that hasn't been tested can't be trusted. Adversity is a watershed—as we suffer heartache, we either give up on God or we cling more tightly to him. There's nothing wrong with asking "Why, God?" But a better question is, "What now?" When we face life's biggest problems, we

> Faith that hasn't been tested can't be trusted.

need to sweep away our shallow misconceptions about God, ask all the hard questions, and still trust his goodness and greatness. Times of suffering expose our faulty beliefs about God and life, and they can lead us into deeper levels of faith if we are willing to trust him and persevere.

Two Houses

All of us need to know our lives count for something far bigger, far more important than our own existence. For centuries, philosophers, poets, novelists, and theologians have pondered the meaning of life. If you've discovered the bigger purpose for your life, that's fantastic. Your faith may look different from mine—or you may not have a faith at all. I'd like to tell you how I've found mine. My intent isn't to convert you to my way of thinking, but to illustrate the innate need for some hope to hold on to when life hurts most.

The Sermon on the Mount is Jesus' best-known message, but many people miss an important aspect of it. Jesus repeatedly pointed to contrasts throughout his teaching: two gates, two roads, two trees, two kinds of fruit, and two motivations to pray, give, and fast. As he closed, he again used one final contrast—this time, of two houses.

> "Everyone then who hears these words of mine and does them will be like a wise man who built his house on the rock. And the rain fell, and the floods came, and the winds blew and beat on that house, but it did not fall, because it had been founded on the rock. And everyone who hears these words of mine and does not do them will be like a foolish man who built his house on the sand. And the rain fell, and the floods came, and the winds blew and beat against that house, and it fell, and great was the fall of it" (Matthew 7:24-27).

Both houses were under attack on all sides. The rains came down, the winds blew laterally, and the floods rose. The houses were battered with no escape and no relief.

The threats were exactly the same for the two houses. Both of them suffered the same intensity, and the storm revealed their different foundations. One of the things we learn from this parable is that a strong faith doesn't protect us from life's storms. Many people expect God to shield them from harm. God sometimes rescues us *from* suffering, but far more often, he rescues us *through* suffering so we learn life's deepest lessons.

We should never see challenges as bad things. After all, we face tests in all aspects of our lives. For example, we use tests to make sure things work correctly. When you buy a new car, you don't wait to test the brakes until you're going 75 miles an hour on a mountain road. You test them in the parking lot, then on the street, and finally on the highway. At each point, your confidence grows that your brakes will work when you need them. In the same

> We should never see challenges as bad things. After all, we face tests in all aspects of our lives.

way, our faith grows as we face (and endure) gradually increasing hardships and setbacks.

What do you have that can't be taken away when trouble strikes? What gives you stability when everything around you is shaken? What is a sure source of light in the darkest days of your life?

You may be casually reading this book, looking for insights and ideas to help discover your purpose in life. That's great, but it's not enough. Sooner or later, your turn will come to face genuine threats to your security and stability. When that day comes, you will only be ready if you've built your life on a firm foundation of faith in Someone who is ultimately wise, kind, forgiving, and strong.

Or you may be reading this book for much the same reason that the crowds went to hear Jesus on the mountain. They may have been a little curious to begin with, but soon discovered that his sermon was both an invitation and a warning. Jesus was thrilled for anyone to experience his love, but he warned his listeners that they could easily miss his point. Being a good person—even a very religious person—was not enough.

The contrasts Jesus drew between the two gates, roads, trees, fruit, and houses weren't comparing good people to bad people, or noble people to evildoers. If we look closely, we see that Jesus was contrasting people who are *trying to prove themselves* with those who are *trusting in*

God's grace. Both groups were motivated do good and noble things. But the first group was trying to impress God with their goodness, and that never works. The second group did good things *in response* to what God had done for them.

Jesus' warning in his concluding story was that we need a stronger foundation for the storms of life than trusting in our morality and talents. We need an infusion of God's forgiveness, kindness, and grace to redirect our motivations, refocus our efforts, and give us the power to stay strong no matter what comes our way.

People seek answers in a variety of places. Personally, I have found mine in Jesus. The message of Christ is counterintuitive. It requires radical exchanges:

- The way to true riches is by giving generously (Luke 6:38);
- The path to greatness is humility (Philippians 2:5-11); and
- True power comes from serving (Matthew 20:25-28).

All of those choices require insight and courage—just like all the exchanges we're addressing in these chapters.

Experiencing this dramatic transformation is essential, but it threatens our pride because we have to trust in God instead of our talents. Regardless of where you are in life, the good news is that it's never too late to change your foundation. When we're rocking along with lots of great friends and meaningful work, we don't think much about the source of

> Sand works fine when there's no storm.

our security. Sand works fine when there's no storm. However, when the rains fall, the winds blow, and the floods rise, we realize the need to sink our pilings deeper into the Rock.

I don't expect people to go to the same church I attend, read the same books about God, pray the same way, and hang out with the same types of people. The kingdom of God is far bigger than any of us can imagine. I'm not even saying that people need to have exactly the same theology I believe. But I am saying this: Sooner or later, we all face devastating circumstances. The storms are coming (if not already here). When we face those inevitable heartaches, our foundations will be exposed. Make sure you build your life on a solid one. Your future, your sanity, and your legacy depend on it.

We need to take an honest look at ourselves. When a house inspector looks at a home that's going up for sale, he carefully examines the foundation. In some parts of the country, drought and floods cause shifts that can create major damage to the walls throughout the house. A poor foundation may be well hidden, yet can create widespread problems.

- If we make pleasure our foundation, we will resent any demands put on us, we will use people to get what we want, and our greatest fear is being bored. We live for excitement and comfort.

- If prestige is our foundation, we'll stay up late at night mentally replaying conversations to think what we might have said differently to impress people more (or avoid looking stupid). We are chameleons, changing our words and behavior to please whoever is in front of us.

- If we live for power, we will insist on always being one up. People will feel used (and often abused). We may be charming one minute but intimidating the next—whatever works to beat the competition.

- If we live to acquire possessions, we will compare everything we own with the latest fashion, technology, cars, houses, and other things our friends have—and we can't stand it until our things are newer than theirs. Even when we get what we want, the joy quickly fades because we worry that someone somewhere has something better.

The problem with these foundations isn't that they *don't quite* cut it; they *can't possibly* hold us up in times of trouble. If we trust them for peace and security, they inevitably deliver disappointment.

You don't have to believe the Bible to acknowledge the ineffectiveness of such foundations. You see people who have built their lives on these things fall to storms every day. We are drawn to things we can see and touch: pleasure, prestige, power, and possessions. They attract us with the allure of control and safety—and in the good times, they seem to deliver what they promise.

The paradox is that the genuine Rock isn't visible or tangible. We see the evidence of God like we see the effects of wind in the trees, yet the invisible God is a firm foundation that not only sustains us during the storms of life but also fills life with his goodness and power. When we exchange shifting sands for solid rock, we acknowledge the weakness of the things we hoped would give us security, and we put all the weight of our hopes and fears in One we can't see. Ultimate security comes as we put our trust in the intangible love and power of God. When he is our foundation, we can stay strong through fierce storms.

In our most lucid moments, we realize we don't live in a bubble. In spite of the glowing ads for products and services that promise to make our lives comfortable, happy, and full of thrills, we know better. Certainly, we have many things to enjoy, but honest perception prevents us from being surprised—and devastated—by the difficulties we experience.

M. Scott Peck observed: "Life is difficult. This is a great truth, one of the greatest truths. It is a great truth because once we truly see this truth, we transcend it. Once we truly know that life is difficult—once we truly understand and accept it—then life is no longer difficult. Because once it is accepted, the fact that life is difficult no longer matters."[19]

EMPTY AND FULL

Tom Brady is one of the greatest NFL quarterbacks who ever played football. He has led the Patriots to three Super Bowl titles and was the game's MVP twice. He's an incredible athlete, he's married to a supermodel, he's handsome, and he makes millions of dollars in salary and endorsements. His teammates love him because he took a lower salary so the team could afford to recruit skilled players from the free agent market, and he often includes his offensive linemen in his endorsement deals so they can make some extra money, too. It would be hard to find anyone who has more of the good life than Tom Brady.

Yet in an interview with *60 Minutes,* Brady dwelled on the stresses of fame. He can't go out to dinner because his fans mob him. Ultimately, all the money and prestige of a superstar athlete have left him feeling confused and empty. He lamented, "How can I have three Super Bowl rings and still think there's something greater out there for me?" He mused that he had reached his highest goals and had every desire fulfilled, but he reflected sadly, "God, there's got to be more than this!"

The interviewer asked, "What's the answer?"

Brady laughed. "I wish I knew. I love playing football, and I love being the quarterback for this team. But at the same time, there are a lot of other parts about me that I'm trying to find."[20]

> Our foundations are usually exposed when we encounter painful circumstances beyond our control.

If Tom Brady's prestige, possessions, power, and pleasure can't fill the hole in his life, how foolish are we to believe we can acquire enough to fill ours?

Our foundations are usually exposed when we encounter painful circumstances beyond our control. Occasionally, though, we can create situations that reveal our foundations. When we first took students to South Africa, we surprised them one morning. At the end of a lecture Garrett told them to go pack their bags for an overnight stay with families who lived in one of the poverty-stricken communities. I was with a young lady named Jessica Grant and several others. We spent the day and the night with a dear family who lived in a tiny shack. When we got back, we asked all the students to describe the lessons they learned from the experience.

Staying with this family revealed to Jessica what was missing in her own life (and in Tom Brady's). Jessica wrote:

During the last 24 hours, living in a small township just outside of Cape Town, I was reminded of what is truly important in life. I grew up in a very close, tight-knit family, and I learned from a very early age how important faith is to one's life. However, when I came to college I was bombarded with a philosophy that tells you to "live it up," "live life to the fullest," and to most of all—focus on yourself during these next four years. And somewhere along the way I bought in to this notion, forgetting a part of my life that was once such a cornerstone of who I was.

Don't get me wrong. I have loved my last three years of college. I have made wonderful friends that will last a lifetime. I have experienced happiness and heartbreak. I have tested my limits, and have learned for myself what is right and wrong. I have at times strayed from my beliefs—but through this, I have experienced personal growth like never before. But, I couldn't help but feel that something was missing in my life.

I think deep down I've always known what this was, but for me it took removing myself from my lifestyle back home, stepping out of my comfort zone, and entering the home of a loving family in South Africa to finally have the courage to open my eyes to what was missing. Back home I was looking for happiness by living it up, living life to the fullest, but it was in this home that I was reminded how different these two things are—and that only one can bring true happiness. For the past three years, I haven't been living life to the fullest, but rather, I have been searching for happiness by "living it up" and focusing on worldly things that I had convinced myself would make me happy.

The family I stayed with this last 24 hours knew what it meant to live life to the fullest. God was so alive in the hearts of this family, and I was reminded of what an amazing refuge the Lord truly is. In the midst of struggle and poverty, this family actively pursues Him in all they do. Their faith is unfailing. And even though they might not have the material luxuries we are accustomed to, the Lord has poured out his blessings on them in a different way. They understand the important things in life like faith, family, friends, and fellowship with those you love. More than anything, this has been a wakeup call for me, and I am leaving this experience strong in knowing how amazing and gracious the Lord is, and humbled by a family who in the midst of struggle always remembers what is truly important in life.

Jessica learned important lessons by watching the faith of others, but some of us learn only by living through our tragedies.

At this point I want to tell you a little more of Ike Reighard's story. Ike grew up in a loving family, and he looked forward to being married and having kids. For twelve years, however, he and his wife Cindy were unable to have children. Infertility can cause enormous stresses in a marriage. The Reighards suffered through monthly disappointments all those years. On their tenth anniversary, Ike gave Cindy a beautiful diamond snowflake necklace and told her, "You're one of a kind, and I love you. If we don't ever have children, that's okay."

Finally, when they were least expecting it, Cindy got pregnant. They were both elated. Ike said, "Family was everything to me, and more than anything, I wanted to be a dad."

After Cindy experienced months of nausea and pain, the day finally came for Ike to take her to Piedmont Hospital for the delivery. Cindy struggled much of the day, so Ike stayed close by her side. A lot of people from their church were in the waiting room. When the nurse examined Cindy again, she announced that the baby would probably be born in about two hours. Cindy felt relieved. For the first time that day, Ike felt free to go out and talk to the people standing vigil. He was gone only about two or three minutes to give them the good news.

As Ike returned through the double doors, he heard a voice on the intercom saying, "Ward 100 to Labor and Delivery." He had no idea what the term meant, but intuitively, he knew something was terribly wrong. He ran down the hall. Cindy's room was just past the next set of double doors. As Ike burst through the doors, a nurse was running from Cindy's room toward the nurses' station. She frantically called out, "My God, somebody needs to come to help! I don't know what's wrong!"

Ike ran into Cindy's room. Immediately, the room filled with doctors, nurses, and crash carts. Several of them turned their attention from Cindy to Ike to ask him to leave the room. He backed into a corner so the team could focus all their attention on Cindy, but he wasn't going to leave her. As he watched the frenetic activity, he thought, *In a minute, I'm going to wake up. This is only a dream. I'm going to roll over and tell Cindy I've just had the worst nightmare of my life.*

Ike watched for 15 or 20 minutes until the doctor in charge looked over and caught his eye. With no emotion in his voice, the doctor asked, "Do we save your wife, or do we save your baby?"

Ike immediately answered, "Save my wife!"

The doctor turned back to work on Cindy. He got up on the bed, balled his fist, and began pounding on her chest. After a few moments Ike saw that his wife was not responding, and he couldn't stand it any longer. He grimaced and said, "Doctor, would you please stop?"

The doctor nodded. It was over. Cindy and the baby were dead.

Slowly, they all walked out into the hallway. The doctors and nurses were weeping with Ike. Several of them said, "I'm so sorry. We don't know what happened."

Ike wondered, *What is this about, God? Why Cindy? She's a much better person than I am or ever will be. Why didn't you take me and leave her and the baby?* He prayed over her and kissed her face. When they pulled the sheet over her face, the shock of reality hit him like a sledgehammer.

Driving home that day, the sunset seemed to indicate the end of everything good, right, pure, and lovely in his life. He remembers, "I dreaded walking through the door of our house. It was the last place I wanted to be. It was the place of all our hopes, and now it only reminded me of all I had lost."

In the weeks and months that followed, Ike asked the same question everyone who has suffered tragic loss instinctively asks: "Why?" By then the doctors had medical reasons for the death of Cindy and their baby. They discovered Cindy had experienced an amniotic embolism, a rare event that occurs about once in 1.5 million births. It was like a heart attack. But of course, medical explanations weren't spiritually and emotionally satisfying.

The "Why?" question became Ike's obsession, but his confusion only magnified his hurt and anger. He found that the searing pain of loss doesn't drift away; it can't be covered up with "happy talk;" and it won't be crowded out with busyness. In our deepest, most confusing losses, we seldom see the hand of God or feel his presence. During those awful days, we have to trust in the unseen but firm foundation of God's love and compassion.

> During those awful days, we have to trust in the unseen but firm foundation of God's love and compassion.

Ike told me, "Sometimes during those terrible days, Spurgeon's insight was like a shaft of light in my darkness. I couldn't trace God's hand in this tragedy, and I was convinced that I never would be able to understand why it happened. But even in the shattering pain and confusion, I realized I could trust the heart of God. The pain certainly didn't go away, but my days and nights were no longer plagued with anguished questions. I put Cindy, our child, and me into the strong, tender hands of the God who wept at loss, shook with anger when leaders didn't show compassion, and answered the ultimate 'why' question by giving his sinless life for sinners like me."

In time, God showed Ike a passage in Isaiah to give him hope in his hopeless situation:

"I will give you the treasures of darkness
    and the hoards in secret places,
    that you may know that it is I, the Lord,
    the God of Israel, who call you by your name" (Isaiah 45:3)

After the shock wore off and the pain became a little more manageable, Ike realized this was a turning point in his life—a lesson he didn't want to miss. He prayed, "Lord, you are sovereign and loving. Nothing comes into my life unless it passes first though your hand. I don't want to live in resentment and sorrow for the rest of my life. God, teach me to handle my trouble rightly. Help me learn the lessons you want me to learn. Use this tragedy to give me more compassion for others who suffer."

Some people look for a clear cause-and-effect in the events of life. If good things happen, they claim, it's because you've been a good person. If bad things happen, the source must be something bad you've done in your life. Certainly, the principle of sowing and reaping is usually valid, but sometimes, bad things happen that we simply can't understand. Many times we simply have to acknowledge that we live in a fallen world, but we must trust that God is able to weave even the worst of events into something beautiful.

As you consider the exchange from shifting sand to a solid Rock, think about these principles:

- The most common forms of "sand" are pleasure, prestige, power, and possessions, each of which produce a unique drive, a unique fear, and a unique threat.
- Our foundations remain hidden during good times, but heartaches reveal them.
- Storms can come from all directions . . . at the same time.
- Trying to do good things to impress God and/or people is shifting sand and won't provide security during storms.

- The only sure foundation is found in something and Someone bigger than yourself.
- Even the greatest success can ultimately leave us empty.
- Sometimes we get a glimpse of reality by watching how others handle suffering.
- We often find treasures in the darkness from our own suffering.
- Even when we can't trace God's hand, we can trust his heart.
- Don't presume a correlation between cause and effect when experiencing life's storms.
- At least one benefit we gain from suffering is a heart of compassion for others who are going through hard times.

The process of grieving major losses is long, uneven, and excruciating. Some storms are like summer thunderstorms that come and go quickly; others are like monsoons that settle and never seem to end. Whether our darkness lasts a short time or seemingly forever, God will be there in the morning with treasures for us. Our heartaches often reveal how empty our lives have been, and God wants to fill them with things that can truly fulfill us: renewed faith, hope, and love.

> *"When a train goes through a tunnel and it's dark, you don't throw away the ticket and jump off. You sit still and trust the engineer."*
> —Corrie Ten Boom

THINK ABOUT IT ...

What are some storms you and your family have experienced? What did those storms reveal about your foundation?

Describe what happens when people build their lives on pleasure, prestige, power, and possessions. What are the different results when people who trust in such things endure heartache and loss?

What advice would you give Tom Brady when he said, "God, there's got to be more than this"?

What might be some treasures God gives us that are only available after the darkness of suffering, confusion, and grief? Has he given you any of those? If he has, describe how you found them and accepted them.

8

CHAPTER 6

EXCHANGING BEING THE MASTER OF NONE TO BEING THE MASTER OF ONE

"My fully exploited strengths are greater than
my marginally improved weaknesses."
—Andy Stanley

As I mentioned previously, when I was a student I had a tendency to get involved in every possible organization and cause. Everything looked equally important, and every activity had the same claim on my time and energy. Finally, I realized I was overextended—by a long shot—and something had to go. It wasn't that any of the organizations and activities were meaningless, but I had to begin to focus.

Some people don't get involved in anything, for any number of reasons. Maybe they don't care, or are afraid of commitment, or already feel overwhelmed by something going on in their lives. Whatever the cause, they stay on the sidelines as observers.

Many schools and organizations honor involvement to the point that anyone who doesn't participate is labeled a slacker. At Texas A&M, everyone is expected to join something. Those who don't are derisively labeled "the two percenters" because that's the ratio of students who aren't actively involved in some campus activity.

Lack of involvement was never my problem. I'm on the other end of the stick—those who can't say "no" to any activity, responsibility, committee, or cause. Just tell me when to show up, and I'll be there!

When people told me that I was spread too thin, I didn't pay attention. I was having too much fun, and I didn't see any reason to change. I wish I could say my motivation was pure altruism, but that would be a lie. I simply had no incentive to focus on any particular cause . . . until I got involved in UGA HEROs. When I saw how that organization was touching kids' lives, I had an epiphany. Suddenly, *one thing* was more important than all the rest. *One cause* captured my heart. *One pursuit* was worthy of my very best.

When we try to do too many things, we simply can't do much of anything very well. We are participants in everything, but masters of nothing. To be painfully honest, my mix of motives included (and still includes) a fierce competitiveness. Compassion and competition make a strange combination, but they're both part of my mix of motivations. I wanted to touch more kids' lives, and I wanted to raise more money than any other student organization at the university. My competitive bent is the reason I like political campaigns and sports. Both activities keep score. Someone wins, and someone loses. That fact is gas in my engine.

I enjoyed the challenge of competing with other campus organizations. UGA HEROs had been a distant third in fundraising the year before, but I knew we could do a lot better. Our faculty advisor thought I was nuts to set a goal that was four times our previous high, but I saw her caution as just one more challenge. Was I an idealist? Sure. Willing to take risks? Obviously. Novelist Pearl S. Buck observed, "The young do not know enough to be prudent, and therefore they attempt the impossible—and achieve it, generation after generation."[21]

As I revealed in the story about helicopters and cows in Chapter 4, we exceeded our goal. The money we raised enabled us to add far more value to the lives of the kids our organization served. All of our creativity, time, and energy—and now, all of my creativity, time, and energy—was devoted to show love to those kids and make their lives a little better. To make sure we understood our purpose, we drew an organizational chart and flipped it upside down. The kids were at the top, the students raising money were under them, our leaders helped the students succeed, and I was at the bottom. The way I saw it, my only purpose was to serve the people above me, and that included everyone! The only way for us to reach our goal was to get far more students committed to fundraising, and the only way that could happen was for me to be far more focused than I'd ever been in my life.

> To make sure we understood our purpose, we drew an organizational chart and flipped it upside down.

That was the first time I made the exchange from being a master of nothing to being a master of one thing. That exchange wasn't excruciatingly difficult because my passion for one thing gave me the clarity to say "no" to all other competing interests. I no longer went to every campus ministry event; I cut back to one each week. I dropped out of campus politics, and I no longer attended meetings of other organizations. Still, there were moments when it was difficult to say "no" to so many good things in order to say "yes" to my one cause.

Focusing on one thing went against my nature and the habits I had developed over a lifetime. Up to that point, I had never pushed all the chips to the center of the table and gone "all in." In school, I did enough to get decent grades, but no one would have called me a scholar. As a kid involved in karate, I got up to the third belt before I lost interest. I loved playing baseball, but I didn't put in extra time in the batting cage or on the field to hone my skills. I don't think I would have been an exceptional player, but now we'll never know because I never gave myself the chance. All of my life, I had been content to dabble in a lot of things, but I had never locked onto one cause, one interest, one goal.

During the year after my epiphany, I had to make repeated choices to focus on one goal instead of many. I was completely dedicated to raising money for UGA HEROs, but I was still drawn back to all the activities I had attended before. Time after time, people called to invite me to go to a meeting, or I saw a poster on campus, or I got an email from the leaders of those organizations about an upcoming event. Each time, I had to make a choice. Each time, I had to pick one over many.

People all over the world who grow grapes for fine wines know the necessity of pruning. Each kind of grape requires a specific technique, but the principle is the same: growers have to prune back perfectly healthy vines to produce even healthier vines that result in more and better grapes. After a grapevine is pruned, it looks like a dead stump.

Those who aren't familiar with pruning may think the vine grower has made a huge mistake, but he has done exactly the right thing.

The pruning process for a grape grower perfectly describes the need for an exchange to become master of one thing. I was in the process of pruning my life so I could ultimately produce more fruit, but a freshly pruned plant doesn't look so great. When we prune our lives, some people will think we've lost our minds or we don't care anymore. They don't understand that we care more than ever, but our devotion has become more targeted.

The exchange I made was certainly worth it. The University of Georgia has more than 500 organizations on campus, and ours was voted "Organization of the Year." Georgia hosts thousands of events every year, but our finale, the HERO Olympics, was voted "Best Campus Event." It's hard to explain the sense of bone-deep satisfaction I felt when the celebration was over and our 2000 students realized they were part of something really special. It was one of the most gratifying moments of my life. As the crowd left the field that day, one student came up to me grinning ear to ear. She said, "This is the happiest day of my life!" I think we all felt that way. It was an incredible privilege to be part of something so powerful. We had become a team when Coach Mark Richt spoke and encouraged students to get out there and raise as much money as possible. We had become a family when we saw the impact our focused efforts were having on children whose lives had been devastated by a dreaded disease.

SIFTING THE OPTIONS

We can be spread so thin doing a lot of good things that we aren't devoted to one compelling cause, or we can be spread thin doing a lot of meaningless things to fill up the emptiness in our days. We need to keep looking, keep analyzing, keep talking, and keep sifting through all the possibilities until we find the one thing that enflames our passions. It's not about personality types. Even the most stoic or reflective people need some fire to keep them going.

> Most people pursue money and prestige as goals, but no amount of those things can fill the holes in our souls.

We don't find our "one thing" by picking it out of a hat or being lucky by clicking on a particular blog when we're bored one day. Most people pursue money and prestige as goals, but no amount of those things can fill the holes in our souls.

Author Malcolm Gladwell points to three necessary components for people to find satisfaction:

> "Those three things—autonomy, complexity and a connection between effort and reward—are, most people agree, the three qualities that work has to have if it is to be satisfying. It is not how much money we make that ultimately makes us happy between nine and five. It's whether our work fulfills us."[22]

In other words, the one thing we choose to pursue needs to give us freedom to act, enough of a challenge to draw out the best in us, and meaningful relationships.

What fulfills us? The answer to that question is different for each person, and the path to find it may have twists and turns. However, we can identify a few important road signs along the way. We need a confluence of affinity, ability, and opportunity.[23]

Affinity

Affinity is what we enjoy doing. When you have time on your hands, what do you naturally think about? What stirs your creativity? What gives you energy? What is the need that captures you so completely that you can't stand it until it's met? A few people knew the answer to these questions when they were five years old. Most of us need to try a lot of things before we realize which ones are worth investing our hearts. We simply can't afford to waste years on jobs and avocations we don't enjoy and that don't make a difference.

Many people stumble into their affinity. I did. Helping kids affected by HIV/AIDS was nowhere on my radar when I started college. Even after getting involved, it took a while for me to see that I wanted to focus on those people and the organization that served them. In many ways, I borrowed others' passion until it became my own. There's nothing wrong with that. I encourage everyone to find people they respect and tag along to see what makes them tick.

Some people are afraid to go all in with a cause or an organization because they're afraid the initial affinity won't last. In reality, it probably won't. Most of us move from one passion to another in different seasons of life. We may be devoted to a particular cause in high school, a different one in college, and still another when we step into our careers. We may be very involved in kids' sports when our children are little, but after they go to high school or college, we don't coach any longer. We are drawn to something else. When we make a commitment to any organization, we're not necessarily signing the rest of our lives over to them. We can change our minds later. People change, organizations change, and passions change.

Another aspect of affinity is that people are not one-dimensional. We can have a different passion (or a few) for each of the aspects of our lives: family, career, hobbies or sports, and friendships. It helps if those passions dovetail in some ways. They may not. But if we're going to make a big difference, we can't be involved in too many things. We need to focus on the few that matter most.

Ability

Our affinities will create frustration if they aren't backed up by our abilities. Some leaders recommend, "Find your passion and pursue it!" That's great advice, but only if the person has talent in that area. I've known some people who spent years trying to succeed in roles where they had very little aptitude. Hobbies are one thing. It's fine to enjoy playing golf or tennis even if you're not good at it. But in a career, it's crucial to match your abilities with your affinity. For example, I love baseball but my abilities are, to say the least, less than stellar. It remains an enjoyable pastime for me. If I couldn't live unless I played for a Major League team, I would be the most frustrated and confused person on earth.

A few people have exemplary skills but little interest in using them. Suppose Joe graduates at the top of his class in accounting, but can't conceive of sitting in an office for the rest of his life. People with abilities that don't match their affinities need to be creative in looking for a solution. In Joe's case, maybe he can teach accounting, or he could start a new business to provide resources for other accountants. He shouldn't assume he is doomed to a life of endless drudgery trying to use his talents in a role he despises.

Opportunity

If a person has a particular passion and the talent to make a difference, we would hope doors of opportunity open for her. They usually do, but not always. An economic downturn can limit job openings, family responsibilities may require time and attention, or something else could get in the way of finding a good fit for her skills.

Sometimes we simply have to pay our dues and wait our turn. I know plenty of mid-level executives who have a passion to lead their division . . . and their company. They have tons of ideas, and they see the flaws in senior management strategies. If they push too hard, however, they may alienate their bosses, or worse, get fired. They need to work diligently and speak selectively. They may have to put in several years before the doors open to them, but they'll be ready when that opportunity comes.

Or there's another solution: when doors are closed to us, we can create new opportunities. My friends could be sending out résumés, talking to headhunters, and networking with contacts. Or they could go to the next level and consider starting their own business or nonprofit organization. It's true that many such businesses fail, but failure isn't the end. Entrepreneurs learn valuable lessons from failure, and the biggest lesson is to never give up on a dream.

Even when affinity, ability, and opportunity converge, we may still struggle with competing desires. The easy, pleasant, fun life looks so attractive, but in our hearts we know it will satisfy only temporarily. We long for something more. E.B. White, the author of *Charlotte's Web*, commented on this tension: "If the world were merely seductive, that would be easy. If it were merely challenging, that would be no problem. But I arise in the morning torn between a desire to improve the world and a desire to enjoy the world. This makes it hard to plan the day."[24]

CENTER OF THE TARGET

If you've read this far, you've shown that you aren't willing to settle for comfort, pleasure, and popularity. You want your life to count.

> If you've read this far, you've shown that you aren't willing to settle for comfort, pleasure, and popularity. You want your life to count.

Blending affinity, ability, and opportunity can be a challenge, but don't quit until you've found what you're looking for. I believe there are concentric circles of our focus. We may be passionate about many things, but only a few meet the three-fold test of affinity, ability, opportunity—and a fourth: the chance to improve the world. Hobbies, clubs, and sports may meet the first three criteria, but they don't belong in the center of the target unless our involvement changes lives.

The principle of focus applies to individuals, families, organizations, and multinational companies. Jack Welch, the former Chairman and CEO of General Electric, described a time when he realized his company was spread too thin. He carefully analyzed the divisions and products in the massive operation, and he decided to close several divisions. What made his decision so difficult was that all of the divisions were profitable, yet several were not aligned with the most important aspects of his company.

And if you think CEOs of companies have trouble ruthlessly pruning products and activities that aren't in the center of their target, nonprofits have an even harder time being focused. HERO for Children is an organization focused solely on quality-of-life care. To accomplish that goal HERO created mentoring programs and conducted one-day special events. Yet people were always coming up with all kinds of other worthwhile ideas about how to help kids. They suggested that HERO provide medical care, food, clothing, and other basic needs. Those weren't bad ideas, and the people who come up with new ideas are usually the ones who are most committed to the cause. But those additional responsibilities would have diluted our focus. We had to keep the most important thing in the center of the target.

"Mission drift" is a threat to thriving businesses and nonprofits. Success always multiplies opportunities, but we have to be wise enough to say "no" when we need to—which is often. Businesses have to maintain a focus on their core products and customers, nonprofits have to avoid adding too many good programs that gradually erode the clarity of their mission, and churches can muddy their message if they say "yes" to the hundreds of ideas for new ministries.

Very few people innately know their focus before they go to college or have their first job. More of us undergo a process of discovery. We change majors, try different jobs, and finally (hopefully) land on a career that is satisfying and makes a difference. In recent decades, several effective tools have been developed to provide insight about people's affinity, ability, and opportunity. If you haven't used any of these tools, I encourage you to take some time to examine them. They'll give you insights and objective input about your personality, interests, skills, and relationships. If you've used one of these instruments in the past and then stuck it in a drawer, take it out again and look at it. Use it as a reference as you make decisions about clarifying your focus.[25]

Another important source of input is feedback from those who know you best. Even if you've used a variety of assessment tools, ask people for their honest appraisal of your strengths and the areas where you can improve. They will probably confirm much of the input you've gotten from the instruments, but sometimes the people who see us regularly can offer considerably more insight than an online test. Of course, we need to be aware of the motives of the person providing the feedback. Some people have an agenda, so we need to listen shrewdly. Be wise and be open, and always be a great listener.

In my experience, there is not a single, foolproof method of determining your strengths. Gather input from many different sources, and look for patterns. If you think you're terrific at a particular skill, but your boss and your peers agree it's not a strength, you may need to do some soul searching. Or maybe your problem isn't misperception, but lack of courage. Some people allegedly continue to search to find their passion although they already know quite well how their affinity, ability, and opportunity line up. But when they look at the changes they will have to make to follow their dream, while saying "no" to many other good things in their lives, they just don't have the courage to take that big step.

Courage can make an enormous impact. Rosa Parks was a complete unknown in Montgomery, Alabama, in 1955. Yet when she refused to move to the back of the bus after the driver insisted she give up her seat for a white passenger, her single act of courage sparked a revolution in the United States. Her simple, bold, focused decision launched a bus boycott and the career of Martin Luther King, Jr. When asked about her experience, she commented, "You must never be fearful about what you are doing when it is right."

Change doesn't happen by magic. It occurs when courageous people make decisions and take action—in careers, social justice, volunteering, family relationships, and every other part of life.

RUTHLESS CHOICES

Previous generations didn't have a wide range of opportunities. No matter what those people were passionate about or skilled at doing, they tended to do what their parents and grandparents had done before them. Things are different today. We have incredible opportunities to try almost anything.

Focusing on a few things instead of spreading ourselves thin is a risk, but life is much more exciting when we step outside our comfort zones. That's when the adrenaline starts pumping. That's when we're most creative. That's when we depend on each other more than ever. Plots without risk don't make great stories. Movies without drama are shown in empty theaters.

And boldness promises great rewards. I've never seen anyone who has found the courage to try something new, has experienced success, and then regrets it! But you can never experience that degree of success without first embracing the risk. You have no guarantees when you step out and give something a try, but I can guarantee boredom if you don't.

No aspect of life is off limits to an analysis of focus. Obviously, we first think of our careers, but we also need to focus our money, our time, and our energy. And patience is essential as we determine our focus. New clusters of grapes don't appear overnight on a pruned vine. Growth takes time, so we shouldn't expect instant results—even if affinity, ability, and opportunity all line up really well. And by "lining up really well," I'm talking about a 70 percent level of satisfaction. You're not going to find a role—in a career, volunteering, marriage, parenting, or anywhere else—that's 100 percent fulfilling. If your set of responsibilities is 70 percent meaningful and 30 percent drudgery, you've hit a home run. If it's better than that, it's a grand slam!

When everyone on a team or in a family appreciates each other, incredible things can happen—and it's a lot more fun. If we happen to be working on the 30 percent of our responsibilities that we'd rather not have to do, like administrative details at work or cleaning the bathroom at home, we should value the skill and dedication of others who perform those tasks all day every day.

When some people get less than exemplary marks in certain areas during a performance review, they determine to focus on those weaknesses more than anything else. Big mistake! Smart workers know their strengths and pour their efforts into maximizing them. No one will remember if you make incremental improvement in an area of weakness, but you might change the world if your strengths become even stronger.

Dale Carnegie, Stephen Covey, and other leadership experts have told a story about two men who sawed timber. Both were determined, hard workers. The first man's saw became dull during the day, but he kept sawing. The second man's saw also became dull, but he stopped to sharpen it. By the end of the day, the second man had cut much more wood than the first. The meaning of the parable is clear: take time to sharpen your saw—your life and your skills. You'll be much more effective if you invest time and resources to improve your greatest strengths.

The most successful people in business, athletics, diplomacy, music, teaching, coaching, engineering, and every other field have poured themselves into one thing. We are successful only when affinity, ability, and opportunity converge. People who make a difference find a way—often through a winding path—for those three things to come together in their lives.

It's easy, though, to drift even after achieving great success. Many basketball fans say that Michael Jordan is the greatest to ever play the game. His highlight reel takes hours to watch. He led the Chicago Bulls to a "three-peat" championship in '92, '93, and '94, but at the height of his fame and skills, Jordan got bored. He decided to give up basketball and try to make it in Major League Baseball. He signed a minor league contract with the Chicago White Sox, who sent him to the Double-A Birmingham Barons. His time with the Barons, though, was disappointing. He batted only .202. He had 30 stolen bases, but he committed 11 errors. His outstanding basketball skills didn't help him learn what every Major League batter has to master—how to hit a curve ball.

While Jordan played for the Barons, the Bulls retired his number 23 jersey and erected a statue to him. His failure in baseball, though, reignited his competitive fires. He decided to return to the Bulls and play again. Amazingly, he hadn't missed a step. He led the team to another three-peat ending in 1998. In his first basketball career, Jordan had laser focus on winning championships, and he was the best in the game. For a short time, he lost his focus, but he had the good sense to admit failure. His return was just as triumphant and even more amazing than his earlier championships. In baseball, Jordan had affinity and opportunity, but not as much ability as he needed. In basketball, he is a human highlight reel for what happens when all three come together.

To make the exchange from being the master of nothing to become a master of one thing, think about these principles:

- We can be spread too thin by doing too many good things or by doing too many meaningless things.

- When we say "yes" to one goal, we're saying "no" to countless others.

- Pruning a life is like pruning grapevines. It looks odd at first, but it produces much more fruit.

- Money and popularity can't ultimately satisfy, and they don't change the world. For that reason, they make very poor goals.

- Your affinity targets the things that arouse your interests.

- Your ability has to do with your strengths and talents.

- Some opportunities are wide open doors, but others require you to create open doors.

- A 70 percent fit is really good, but we can keep pushing to make our pursuits even more fulfilling.

- Assessment tools and feedback give us insight and clarity about our direction.

- Invest more in maximizing your strengths than in improving your weak areas.

- When you make a bold decision to be a master of one thing (or a few things), you can expect doubts and pushback.

- The only guarantee is that if you don't make ruthless decisions to focus your time and energy, you will live a boring and empty life.

Focusing on the things that matter means going all in. When you reorient your focus, expect internal and external opposition. You may have second thoughts about your decision, and your doubts are likely to be reinforced by a chorus of voices shouting that you're doing the wrong thing. Some critics will shake their heads and walk away; others will find delight in pointing out every little thing that goes wrong—to you

People who try bold things inevitably encounter opposition.

and to everyone else who will listen. People who try bold things inevitably encounter opposition. Don't be surprised, and don't back down. If you want to accomplish the impossible, you need to prepare to be uncomfortable.

> *"Once you say you're going to settle for second, that's what happens*
> *to you in life."*
> —*John F. Kennedy*

THINK ABOUT IT . . .

On a spectrum from 0 (spread too thin) to 10 (really focused), how would you rate yourself at this point in your life? Explain your answer.

Describe your affinity, your ability, and your opportunity. Are they clear? Are they converging? Why or why not?

Why is pruning important? How does it work? How can you see it working in your life? How long does it take before new growth and fruit become evident in a person's life?

What are some ways you can invest in your strengths? What will be some of the benefits?

8

CHAPTER 7

EXCHANGING ACCEPTANCE FOR ACCOMPLISHMENT

"The opposite of courage is not cowardice; it's conformity."
—*Jim Hightower*

*M*aybe we were idiots. I'm sure a lot of people thought so. After ADDO had been operating for a couple of years, Hall of Fame Coach Vince Dooley nominated us for the Governor's International Award for the best "New Company of the Year." The *Atlanta Business Chronicle* hosts the annual awards. Hundreds of new companies were nominated in our category, and we were one of five finalists.

My business partner Garrett and I realized we were out of our league. The other nominees for awards were closing business deals worth billions. We were doing leadership conferences for students in several countries and consulting with orphanages in Indonesia. It seemed absurd to even be in the same room with some of the most seasoned and skilled business people in our state, but Coach Dooley believed in us.

We had no expectations of winning, but we decided we wanted to do something memorable if by some faint chance we heard our names called. A few months before, Garrett and I had chaired a conference in Romania for young leaders from 30 European countries. At the week-long event, we had time to get to know people. One student in particular impressed me, and I had the opportunity to really get to know her. Paula told me about her mom, whom she loves very much, but her mom isn't able to provide for her family. She also told me of her father who isn't involved in her life, other than an occasional phone call and sending small amounts of money. Paula even told of her grandmother who helped raise her and remains an inspiration to her. I've met amazing individuals around the world, but Paula was special. I believed Paula had the ability to change the world—she just needed some hope. When I told her about the possibilities of making a difference, she believed I was overly optimistic . . . and maybe a little naïve. She questioned the American ideal of a "right to pursue happiness." After the conference, Garrett and I concluded that if there was ever a way to make it happen, we wanted her to experience America. We wanted to find the money to fly Paula over to spend some time with us and expand her horizons.

The awards ceremony was the perfect opportunity. One of the sponsors of the awards was Delta Airlines, and the keynote speaker would be Delta's CEO, Richard Anderson. If we won, we were going to make a blatant, shameless, full-on pitch to Delta to give Paula a roundtrip ticket. We wanted to meet with someone from Delta to ask for the ticket. But first, we had to make an impression.

Before the event, the organizers told all the nominees that the winners were to come up to the stage, receive the award, say "Thank you," have a picture taken, and walk off. There was no time for a speech of any kind. That limitation, we realized, would ruin our chance to connect with Mr. Anderson. We still didn't think we had much of a chance to be the ones standing on the platform during the presentations, but if it happened, we were determined to risk our reputations to make a statement.

After Richard Anderson spoke, he sat at a table in front of the platform. We were at a table with our parents and the Dooleys. The first award was for our category: New Company of the Year. I had seen enough Oscar shows to know that everyone nominated looks conflicted in the moment before the winner's name is spoken. Now I understood why. The seconds dragged by. It seemed they would never announce the winner. In those eternal moments, I thought about winning, losing, winning again, and losing again. Finally, we heard our names! Garrett and I looked at each other and nodded . . . Show time! We were ready for the performance of our lives.

> We had written and rehearsed something like a *Saturday Night Live* skit that used every marketing slogan in Delta's history. I was the straight man.

We took the award, stopped and smiled for pictures, and then stepped to the microphone. We weren't going to stop with "Thank you." We had written and rehearsed something like a *Saturday Night Live* skit that used every marketing slogan in Delta's history. I was the straight man.

First we told the audience that our goal was to "score a meeting with Delta CEO Richard Anderson." I said, "We do leadership training around the world where we inspire people, equip entrepreneurs, and partner with local businesses and NGOs. We've gone to six continents." Garrett then leaned in and added: "Which reminds me of the reach of Delta Airlines, which serves more than 900 cities around the world. That's right. Delta's ready when you are."

Next we thanked our parents, Vince and Barbara Dooley, Senator Johnny Isakson, and the hosts from the *Atlanta Business Chronicle*. I said, "There are many others who helped us get to this point tonight." Garrett jumped in: "Which reminds me of our friends at Delta Airlines. Delta, keep climbing!"

I gave a synopsis of Paula's inspiring story. She had grown up in Romania, a beautiful country with wonderful traditions, but with very little hope. Paula worked to support herself and her mother, and still made straight A's in school.

I explained that we realized Paula couldn't have afforded the registration fee for the conference where we met her. She explained that she and a friend had worked on a conference planning committee with the promise of getting to go for free. However, funds were unexpectedly tight and the offer was rescinded a couple of weeks before the conference began. Paula was heartbroken, but a few days later she was told that an anonymous donor had given money to provide a scholarship for her.

She would later discover that her friend was the anonymous donor. The friend asked his parents to give him money for his birthday, Christmas, and any other present they would give him for the next year so *he* could go to the conference. His plan was to leave home each day and return after the last meeting had ended. He didn't want his parents to know his plan, and he didn't want Paula to know he had paid her way. It was a conspiracy of love.

Before Garrett and I left the conference to go home, Paula gave us a handwritten note saying that ADDO had inspired her to keep reaching toward her dreams. Romania has a rich cultural heritage, but decades of Communist domination have crushed hope out of the people. Of all of the places I've been, it may very well be the most hopeless. I had assured Paula that things aren't always great in America, but it is, in fact, a land of unbounded optimism.

After I briefly chronicled Paula's story at the awards ceremony, we asked Delta for a plane ticket for her. Garrett told the audience, "There are people like Paula all over the world. They have potential, but they need a push. Ability is spread equally across society, but opportunity is not. With ADDO, we have the opportunity to inspire people today so they will impact tomorrow. We want to reach more people around the world. Our possibilities are only limited by our partnerships."

In the meantime the incredulous host had been frantically motioning for us to shut up and sit down. But we weren't quite finished. I told the crowd, "And speaking of partnerships . . ." Garrett and I put on pilots' hats and said in unison, "Like our friends at Delta, we love to fly, and it shows!"

The editor of the *Atlanta Business Chronicle* was visibly distressed, but he couldn't say much because we got a standing ovation. After we sat down, we got word that Richard Anderson wanted to see us. Delta gladly offered to fly Paula to Atlanta. We wished we could have brought

20 gifted young leaders from Romania to America, but we wanted to have an impact on at least one.

Our quirky presentation turned out well, but it could have gone badly . . . very badly. We knew we were taking a huge risk, and our reputations could have been tarnished for a long time. But we were willing to exchange acceptance to accomplish a much bigger goal: having an impact on a young lady in Romania who had shown incredible bravery, vision, and kindness.

Go Along to Get Along

Daring to be different can create a host of problems. When we try something big and new, we often feel awkward and unsure of ourselves, and we are afraid any failure will define us for too long. But those messages aren't only in our heads. When we dare to attempt something big and new, it makes other people feel uneasy and they don't mind saying so. They often try to remedy their discomfort by forcing us to get back in line. They may assume we've lost our minds and say, "You're nuts!" Or worse, they can accuse us of being selfish because we don't follow the same path they do. To those entrenched in safety and security, being different looks like arrogance.

> Daring to be different can create a host of problems.

And there are always naysayers. Some people listen to our dreams and instantly conclude, "It'll never work. Why would you even try that?" Some understand the goal we're trying to achieve, but they can't believe that the method could ever be productive. They complain,

"That's not the way anybody else is doing it. It has never been done that way before, so you'd better think about it again. Don't do something you'll regret!" Actually, I don't think they're worried about what we will regret. They're more concerned that they will somehow be splashed with the dark paint of failure if our crazy plans don't succeed . . . or covered with the green of envy if they do.

Steve Jobs was an idiosyncratic genius who changed the way the world communicates. At every point in his remarkable career at Apple, people told him he couldn't possibly turn his crazy ideas into reality. He consistently proved them wrong. He articulated his philosophy in a bold, dramatic statement:

> "Here's to the crazy ones. The misfits. The rebels. The trouble-makers. The round pegs in the square holes. The ones who see things differently. They're not fond of rules. And they have no respect for the status quo. You can quote them, disagree with them, glorify or vilify them. About the only thing you can't do is ignore them. Because they change things. They push the human race forward. And while some may see them as the crazy ones, we see genius. Because the people who are crazy enough to think they can change the world, are the ones who do."[26]

The role of leadership requires the exchange of pleasantries for purpose—to achieve something far bigger and better than popularity. Leaders don't have to be weird, and they realize there is no inherent value in being obnoxious. But if you're a leader, you will sometimes feel like you're going over the brink of risk and loneliness. When you lead people, you will alienate a few, but inspire many more. We have to be willing to suffer the barbs of the few for the sake of the many. French fashion designer Coco Chanel commented, "In order to be irreplaceable, one must always be different."[27] And being different makes us lightning rods.

It may seem odd and obvious to say it, but leaders lead. At the most basic level, leadership involves stepping out and inviting others to follow. Real leaders aren't like politicians who take opinion surveys of their constituents before deciding how to vote on a bill. They listen to people, but they're willing to follow their convictions even if people disagree. People are looking for leaders who have a clear vision and the courage of their convictions. We admire people in any walk of life who step away from the masses and point the way to a better future. R.S. Donnell rightly observed, "The man who follows a crowd will never be followed by a crowd."[28] And entrepreneur Seth Godin commented, "If you're remarkable, it's likely that some people won't like you."[29]

A few leaders thrive on controversy: the hotter the condemnation, the better they like it. I don't think many are like that. I'm certainly not. Stepping out, though, is always uncomfortable to some extent. When we exchange acceptance for accomplishment, we leave behind the comfort of the crowd. We abandon the status quo and reach for more and better options. We may feel every bit as unsure of our course as those who shake their heads at us, but we're determined to give change a shot.

The acceptance of others is always a moving target. If we live to win others' approval, they soon learn that we're like puppets on a string. They can make us dance by pulling the strings of praise or criticism.

Everything we do and say is designed to win the smiles of those we want to impress. When we get the acceptance we crave, we feel on top of the

> The acceptance of others is always a moving target.

world. When it is withheld, we review conversations to figure out what went wrong, and we change our words, values, and actions to please our critics. Steven Furtick noted, "He who lives by the approval of others will die by the absence of same."[30] And actress Celeste Holm painfully observed, "We live by encouragement and die without it—slowly, sadly, angrily."[31]

I'm not suggesting that relationships aren't important. We have a universal need to love and be loved. Psychologists tell us that emotional health—and even life itself—requires meaningful human connections. But the same experts warn that our lives become ingrown, shallow, and sick if we don't combine meaningful relationships with a driving, dynamic purpose in life. The two go hand in hand. Leaders are those who have figured out how to blend the two, and they know that accomplishment means nothing if it's not saturated in relationships—inspiring people to follow and achieve the goal, and benefiting people with the accomplishment of the goal.

Acceptance certainly isn't wrong, and the desire for affirmation isn't evil or immature. But when the thirst for approval consumes us and prevents us from pursuing our dreams, it's out of balance and needs correction. At that point, we need to make the exchange. We were put here for a reason. We have the privilege and the responsibility to make a difference.

Acceptance is attractive; rejection is excruciating. Living on the treadmill of pleasing people to earn a sense of security, though, is a dead end. We need good and healthy relationships. We can't make it without them. However, some of us may not know what healthy relationships look like. Here's a measuring stick: you can know your connections are strong when your friends celebrate your courage to step out and take risks instead of ridiculing you.

Don't let the fear of what others think about you prevent you from being all you can be and fulfilling your destiny.

Stay Out of the Basket

I have heard stories from several speakers about the strange behavior of crabs, used to illustrate the liabilities of going along with the crowd. On the East Coast and Gulf Coast, people often catch blue crabs to cook in crab cakes, gumbos, and sauces. One technique of catching crabs involves tying a chicken leg on a string and tossing it into the water. When a nice fat crab latches onto the chicken leg, it won't let go—even when the fisherman pulls it out of the water into the netherworld of air and light. Crab fishermen also say that the first crab caught desperately tries to crawl out of the basket, so they have to keep a lid on it. After a few more crabs are added to the basket, however, something very strange happens: the crabs no longer try to climb out. If one tries to get out, the others grab it and drag it back. The community of trapped crabs feels comfortable with each other, so most of them sit peacefully in the bottom of the basket.

The principle of the crab basket can be observed in businesses, clubs, nonprofits, churches, and networks of friends. When people are alone, they often try new things, but a crowd often has a dampening effect on creativity and ingenuity. In the comfort of familiar relationships, people seldom take risks, and they thrive on mediocrity. They seldom think "outside the basket." They may angle for a promotion to be "king crab," but they're still in the confined universe of the crab basket. Everyone in the organization has a role and a position: some on top, some on the bottom, and a lot in between. It doesn't take many crabs (or people) to become myopic and believe the whole world exists inside the basket. Gradually, going *outside* appears more threatening than being *inside.* Any attempts to climb out are met with multiple arms and claws grabbing and pulling the adventurous person back down. Staying in the basket with other crabs feels familiar, appears safe, and avoids conflict.

Any risks involved in climbing out of the basket are worth it. The world is full of dangers, of course, and nothing is guaranteed. Yet although the crab basket seems a lot safer, one guarantee is that sooner or later most of those crabs are going into a boiling pot and onto someone's dinner table!

The best advice is to avoid getting lured into the basket in the first place because life happens outside the crab basket. We don't have to be crabs. We can choose to stay outside with a few dangers and many unknowns . . . but unlimited possibilities. Freedom, joy, and potential all abound outside and away from the crowd.

We can exchange acceptance for accomplishment at various levels of life, but it's always a challenge. We value acceptance for different reasons, depending on where we are. We may want social acceptance to fit in with our friends and family, or we may desire organizational acceptance to gain prestige and a higher position. Of course, most of us are *always* seeking acceptance, especially by the time we get out of school and enter the working world.

Students have to make dozens of such choices every day. When they see someone being bullied, do they stand around and watch because they are afraid of being next on the hit list, or do they stand up for the victim? When they hear peers verbally ripping another person to shreds with vicious gossip, do they join in because they want to be one of the crowd, or do they refuse to participate and walk away?

In college, when professors teach aspects of philosophy or theology that contradict students' beliefs, do they parrot back the professor's perspective just to get a good grade, or do they at least include a paragraph stating that they understand the points but just don't agree? In a world that puts a premium on "tolerance" but is intolerant of anyone with a defined faith, do they reluctantly concede that every belief and behavior is equally valid, or do they have the courage to take a stand on truth that may offend some people?

In the business environment, the exchange takes on a different form, but it's just as real. Do we inaccurately inflate our résumés to get better jobs, or do we tell the truth about our grades and work experience? Do we shamelessly promote our achievements to others, or do we let our performance do the talking—at the risk of seeing ladder-climbers promoted ahead of us? Do we engage in divisive office politics that spread rumors about the integrity and work of a colleague, or do we mind our own business and do our jobs well?

In a family, do we avoid hard conversations because certain relatives intimidate us with their anger, or are we willing to risk expressing our true feelings and hope that something good may come out of honesty?

I'm under no illusions that things will always work out just fine when we make this exchange. Quite often, people accuse us of being stupid or selfish, we're branded as outsiders, we don't get the promotion, or we are ignored. In the short term, we usually catch flak—sometimes, lots of flak. If people have previously manipulated us with anger, whining, or cold shoulders, they will double their efforts if they sense we're determined to change the nature of the relationship. It's tempting to give in and avoid conflict. But consciously exchanging acceptance for accomplishment gives us a new purpose, new courage, and a new plan. Sooner or later, our consistent, new behavior changes those shaky relationships. Other people may not agree with our course of action, but we gradually earn their respect.

We need to make this exchange in small ways dozens of times every day, and probably a few major times in our lives. When you exchange acceptance for accomplishment, people notice. They want to understand your motivation for stepping away from the crowd, and they want to see how you handle opposition. They secretly want to make the exchange, too, but they need a role model. Our choices have a ripple effect, often far beyond our immediate relationships.

> When you exchange acceptance for accomplishment, people notice.

Billy Graham once said, "Courage is contagious. When a brave man takes a stand, the spines of others are often stiffened."[32]

One of my heroes is Ronald Reagan. Regardless of political affiliations, most people can appreciate his vision and courage. He often faced fierce opposition, not only from members of the other party, but even from his closest aides.

By 1987, the Cold War had been freezing Europe for over four decades. Germany had been divided since the Nazis surrendered and Allied armies occupied the area in May of 1945. East Germany became a satellite of the Soviet Union while West Germany had considerably more freedom. For a few years, travel between East and West Germany was allowed, but in 1961 the Communists erected a concrete wall in Berlin to separate the two. The wall was topped with barbed wire and had strategically positioned machine gun emplacements.

When Reagan became President, he worked shrewdly with Mikhail Gorbachev, the General Secretary of the Communist Party of the Soviet Union. They initially agreed to several groundbreaking treaties to limit nuclear proliferation, but in 1987, tensions rose again over the Americans stationing short-range missiles in Europe and building up the U.S. armed forces.

After an economic summit in Venice, Reagan traveled to Berlin to make a point. He wanted to speak at the Brandenburg Gate, a symbolic site of the former unity—and now the separation—of Germany. The Berlin Wall stood as an ugly scar across the city, the nation, and the world.

As Reagan and his associates wrote his speech, he liked the clarity and power of a single line inviting Gorbachev to finally "tear down this wall." Some of his closest advisors, however, felt the statement was too inflammatory, especially in the rising tensions of the moment. Howard Baker, his Chief of Staff, and Colin Powell, the National Security Advisor, told him the line sounded "extreme" and "unpresidential." Reagan considered their advice, but he had a different agenda. The world was watching, and Reagan didn't care that he might ruffle a few feathers. He believed the time was right to issue a challenge to the Soviet leader who had his hand on the leaders of East Germany.

Reagan stepped up to the platform at the Brandenburg Gate on the afternoon of June 12. Two panes of bulletproof glass shielded him from snipers over the wall in East Germany. The President's speech provided a framework for democracy and unity in that troubled country. At the conclusion, he spoke with conviction:

"We welcome change and openness; for we believe that freedom and security go together, that the advance of human liberty can only strengthen the cause of world peace. There is one sign the Soviets can make that would be unmistakable, that would advance dramatically the cause of freedom and peace. General Secretary Gorbachev, if you seek peace, if you seek prosperity for the Soviet Union and Eastern Europe, if you seek liberalization, come here to this gate. Mr. Gorbachev, open this gate. Mr. Gorbachev... Mr. Gorbachev, tear down this wall!"[33]

The crowd erupted in shouts and applause. Reagan had spoken the impassioned sentiment in the heart of every German—East or West. He hadn't just given a brilliant speech on foreign policy. He challenged Gorbachev, the one person with the power to make a difference, to stand up and do something dramatic.

In response, it took just over two years to bring down a symbol of oppression that had stood for four decades. Gorbachev authorized removal of the Berlin Wall, and on November 9, 1989, the people of

Berlin used sledgehammers, picks, and bare hands to tear it down. The most important four words in Reagan's presidency had made a difference. With political insight and an understanding of humanity's thirst for freedom, he dared to issue a public invitation and bold challenge to Gorbachev. Reagan defied his closest advisors, and he risked raising tensions with an old foe. He was willing to endure any repercussions the media and historians might dish out. He made the exchange, and the world took another step toward freedom.

Consider these principles as you make the exchange from acceptance to accomplishment:

- Conformity is doing what everyone else does, regardless of what is right. Integrity is doing what is right regardless of what everyone else is doing.
- We face dozens of opportunities to make this exchange every day.
- Acceptance comes in two forms: relational and organizational. Both are seductive, and both require exchanges.
- We need to blend and balance acceptance and accomplishment. We get into trouble when the desire to fit in drowns the desire to make a difference.
- When we make this exchange, we usually experience self-doubt and opposition. But if we consistently make this exchange, we earn the respect of people who are watching.
- Stay out of the crab basket. If you're in it, get out!

The results of exchanging acceptance for accomplishment are seldom as dramatic as Reagan's "Tear down this wall!" speech, but even small exchanges add up to make a big difference in our lives and in the lives of those who are watching us.

At the conference in Romania where Garrett and I met Paula, one of the speakers told the audience, "People don't change the world; events change the world." As it happened, Garrett was the very next speaker. He told the audience, "I completely disagree with what the last speaker said. People—those with vision and courage—are the only hope for the world. People shape events, and therefore, people change the world."

When Paula came to America, we took her to three cities. We first brought her to Atlanta and explained the impact of Martin Luther King Jr. in the Civil Rights Movement. Segregation was a scar on our nation, but Dr. King and many others took bold steps to establish equality in every corner of our country. We took her to Washington, D.C. and told her how a small group of people had incredible foresight and bravery to pull away from Great Britain and launch a new nation. We then took her on a tour of Ground Zero in New York City to demonstrate the resilience of people who suffered the worst blow in American history and have come back even stronger. In each instance, people believed that things could be better, that we had the power to change the destiny of others, and that hope reigns.

We took the risk at the awards ceremony of looking "dumb and dumber," but the risk was worth it in order to accomplish our goal of renewing Paula's hope and vision. We put our reputation at stake for another person. The vast majority of our choices, though, are seldom as big and clear. Dozens of times every day, we face choices—often unnoticed choices—to value making an impact more than winning someone's smile. It's a challenge I have to keep facing over and over, but it's one that will make a huge difference in the impact of my life.

Living for acceptance makes us insecure, erodes our confidence, and makes us easily manipulated by others' smiles or frowns. When we find the courage to pursue accomplishment, we earn respect—even from those who oppose us. Consistently making this exchange establishes a trajectory for our lives that's full of richer relationships because they aren't ends in themselves. We're encouraging each other to reach higher and go farther. We're helping each other stay out of the crab basket.

> When we find the courage to pursue accomplishment, we earn respect—even from those who oppose us.

"If you just set out to be liked, you will be prepared to compromise on anything at anytime, and would achieve nothing."
—*Margaret Thatcher*

THINK ABOUT IT ...

What are the benefits of fitting in and being accepted? What are the risks?

How would you describe the need to balance the desire for acceptance with the drive to accomplish something with your life? How can you tell if they are out of balance and need to be adjusted?

Are you in the crab basket right now? Explain your answer.

What are some exchanges of acceptance for accomplishment you face every day? What are some major ones you have made in the past?

If you make this exchange more consistently, how will you benefit? How will others benefit?

8

EXCHANGING THE IMMEDIATE FOR THE ULTIMATE

"The chief cause of failure and unhappiness is trading
what we want most for what we want now."
—Zig Ziglar

*I*f you've been paying attention throughout this book, I have given you credit for having quite a lot. I have suggested that you have stability, fans, and the acceptance of others. I have credited you with making expedient choices and being involved in a lot of worthwhile things. You already have what many people think would make them happy. And yet I have asked you to give those things up, one by one, in order to exchange each one for something even better.

All of those previous exchanges hinge on this one: exchanging the immediate for the ultimate. Each exchange requires us to give up something in the short term in order to accomplish something greater in the future. Exchanges are based on new priorities, and those priorities necessarily produce bold action. If we don't act, the new priorities are merely good (but impotent) ideas. They haven't yet captured our imaginations and produced choices that change the direction of our lives. As Mahatma Ghandi said, "Action expresses priorities."[34]

However, when we consider choices based on new priorities, we immediately think of dozens of reasons to remain stuck in the status quo. Choices involve sacrifice and risk. We have to give up something we have valued—maybe for years, maybe our whole lives—to reach for something better. We may fail. People may laugh at us. We may invest valuable resources that will be forever lost.

I never want to give the impression that the exchanges I have proposed always lead to a smooth road and fantastic results. They may, but sometimes they won't. The questions you need to ask at each moment of decision are: (1) Is my prospect of gain greater than the assurance of staying stuck where I am? and, (2) Am I willing to sacrifice my present comfort for potential benefits? If not, you won't make any exchanges. But if you take the risks involved with change, you will live a life of adventure and purpose. You will experience both "the thrill of victory and the agony of defeat," and your life will never be boring.

I can't think of a better example of this exchange than my mother. She was the homecoming queen at her high school, and she has always had that rare, enviable combination of beauty and personality. My father has quiet strength, but my mother is a vocal leader. People instinctively look to her for guidance and help.

After my sister and I were born, my mother quit her job to be home with us. By the time Whitney and I had started school, my father's building business was suffering because of the economy. At that point, our family couldn't make it on his fireman's salary alone, so my mother went back to work. She was qualified for a job in sales or management, but she needed work quickly and took a job in the warehouse of Scholastic Books. Every day she strapped on a back support so she could stack cases of books. Was that her dream job? Not in the least. Was it what she wanted? It depends on how you look at it. She wanted to help provide for our family more than she wanted immediate comfort or the gratification of a more satisfying job. So in one way, yes, working in the warehouse was exactly what she wanted. Our family needed the additional income, and she was willing to sacrifice to meet that need.

However, my mother's motivation wasn't just to bring in a few more dollars so we would be a little more comfortable. She had a much bigger goal. No one in our family had ever graduated from college. My parents were committed to earn enough money for my sister and me to get university degrees, and my mother was determined to make this dream become a reality. Later she got a job more tailored to her skills, but for a season she was willing to do hard physical work in the warehouse because she had a vision of a better future for our family—and she never complained. Of course, I didn't understand the sacrifice she was making when I was a little kid. It's only now that I look back—now that I face similar exchanges in my own life—that I appreciate my mother's heart and her courage.

OPTIONS

As I talk with people who are older, I noticed that those who are unhappy with their lives often point back to a particular period (maybe even a specific moment) when they chose comfort in the short term instead of taking a risk to achieve something bigger. Some have told me, "I wish I had it to do over again. I wish I had made a wiser, more courageous choice. My life would be so different today."

Perhaps they wanted to get into grad school, but watched *SportsCenter* or played video games instead of studying. They wanted the job of their dreams, but they weren't willing to do extra work to get the promotion. They wanted to get in shape, but it was easier to eat another slice of pizza and chat with friends. They wanted to invest time in caring for disadvantaged people, but their friends thought they had lost their minds. They wanted to be the very best parents to their little kids, but making more money seemed essential at the time.

> The challenges force us to reevaluate our priorities every day and be ruthlessly honest about what our actions say about our true values.

The examples are endless, and the choices are always hard. The challenges force us to reevaluate our priorities every day and be ruthlessly honest about what our actions say about our true values. We need to reflect on past decisions and note the pattern of our choices. This exchange—and all the others—requires us to sacrifice a little now for the sake of much more later on.

We have a built-in desire for satisfaction, comfort, and ease. It's hard to give those up for the promise of something we can't yet see, feel, hear, taste, and smell. One of the most common reasons people of my generation don't want to make exchanges is the desire to keep their options open. They realize every decision for one thing is a decision against a hundred other possibilities. They instinctively don't want to limit the range of options, so they decide to avoid deciding.

In an article for Forbes about 20-somethings, Jenna Goudreau quotes Dr. Meg Jay, author of *The Defining Decade: Why Your Twenties Matter—and How to Make the Most of Them.* Jay observes that 80 percent of life's most important events happen by the time people are 35, so the 20s are the "developmental sweet spot." Those who keep their options open too long, she warns, will never catch up. Jay says, "These 20-somethings think they are keeping their options open, but they are actually closing doors." Drawing conclusions from Jay's research, Goudreau notes:

> "Reveling in a decade-long identity crisis will not result in better-adjusted adults, she says. Research shows that 20-something unemployment is associated with heavy drinking and depression in middle age—even after becoming regularly employed. Meanwhile, 20-somethings who are underemployed for just nine months tend to be more depressed and less motivated than their peers—even their unemployed peers."[35]

Some of us are goal-oriented, some are highly relational, and some are naturally skilled at organization. Whatever our personality, temperament, talents, and training, all of us naturally gravitate to immediate pleasure and comfort over long-term risks and benefits. We need to realize that today's choices matter. A single decision to pick an immediate pleasure over an ultimate goal may not seem like a big deal, but a thousand of those choices add up.

No Regrets

Bronnie Ware is an Australian nurse who cares for patients during their last 12 weeks of life, commonly known in this country as hospice care. In her conversations with people facing the end of their lives, she recorded the five most common and piercing

> No one regretted missing out on making more money, having better sex, or bungee jumping.

regrets. No one regretted missing out on making more money, having better sex, or bungee jumping.

The top five were:

1. "I wish I'd had the courage to live a life true to myself, not the life others expected of me."

   This, Ware notes, is the most common regret she encountered. Many people looked back on their lives and realized they had lived according to the expectations of others instead of pursuing their own dreams. They were going to die with the painful knowledge they had missed the best life had to offer.

2. "I wish I hadn't worked so hard."

   Ware said that every male patient communicated the pain of choosing work, money, and positions over the people they claimed to love. They missed their children's games and conversations, and their spouse's warmth and laughs. All of them looked back with horror that they had made foolish and selfish decisions to choose work and money over their families.

3. "I wish I'd had the courage to express my feelings."

Many of her patients realized they had chosen to avoid conflict by suppressing their true feelings. The short-term benefits led to long-term resentment, emotional isolation, and permanent strains in relationships. In many cases, the emotional stress contributed to the disease that was killing them. The immediate goal of keeping an artificial peace came at a big price.

4. "I wish I had stayed in touch with my friends."

As people near death, many suddenly realize they have neglected the treasure of wonderful relationships. They may have drifted apart for many different reasons, but they miss the understanding, support, laughs, stories, and shared experiences they enjoyed with their friends.

5. "I wish that I had let myself be happier."

Ware notes, "This is a surprisingly common one. Many did not realize until the end that happiness is a choice. They had stayed stuck in old patterns and habits. The so-called 'comfort' of familiarity overflowed into their emotions, as well as their physical lives. Fear of change had them pretending to others, and to their selves, that they were content, when deep within, they longed to laugh properly and have silliness in their life again."[36]

When we're young, it's easy to dismiss the complaints of older people, but we need to take those regrets seriously. All of those elderly men and women were young once, and they faced the same choices we face today. They look back and wish they had made better decisions when they were our age. In almost all cases, their choices seemed completely reasonable at the time—just like our bad choices seem to us. When we choose the ultimate over the immediate, we may not see the benefits for a while. But later, when we have the benefit of looking in the rearview mirror, we'll realize the importance of making this exchange—and making it often.

INVESTING IN THE FUTURE

To invest in the ultimate instead of the immediate, we first need a clear picture of what we really want. Having a vision of the future gives us four important insights:

- It helps us know where we're going, enabling us to navigate opportunities and threats more effectively.
- It helps us know why we're going in that direction so our purpose can remain clear and strong.
- It helps us remain willing to make daily decisions to choose the ultimate purpose of our lives over immediate comfort.
- It helps keep the flame of passion kindled so that disappointment and opposition don't discourage us.

A compelling vision of a better future changes everything. That's the reason my mother went to work in a warehouse for a while, and that's the reason all of us make choices to let go of immediate gratification and reach for ultimate gains.

In making this exchange, we're swimming upstream against a current of culture that promises instant fulfillment of every need. The messages we hear every day scream that we are entitled to have everything we could possibly want in order to be completely happy . . . now! We get impatient as we wait for the microwave to finish cooking dinner. We can instantly communicate with virtually anyone around

> In making this exchange, we're swimming upstream against a current of culture that promises instant fulfillment of every need.

the world. In fact, we can see them as we talk to them. A generation ago, those conveniences and tools were the stuff of science fiction. When my friends from Europe come to America, they marvel at all the drive-thrus. They have some drive-thru fast-food restaurants in their countries, but they are amazed to see drive-thru banks, pharmacies, and liquor stores!

The culture tells us that the promise of plenty is for right now. We don't have to wait, not even for a few minutes! Gradually, the barrage of messages erodes our patience and our vision for the future.

We need to notice when cultural currents begin to sweep us downstream with expectations of instant gratification. That's when we most need to resist and work hard to create a new set of values and a more robust mental framework that values sacrifice. Yes, I realize it sounds really strange to say we value sacrifice. Yet far too often we settle for second best. We're content with having a little now, but we don't realize that we're mortgaging our future. The only way to make any or all of the exchanges in this book is to live for long-term benefits more than short-term comfort. If there's nothing out there that captures our hearts, we won't make this exchange—or any of the others.

If we see only the choice right in front of us, our natural instinct is to choose whatever makes us happier right now. If, though, we zoom out far enough to see our lives in the future and what we could potentially accomplish, we create an effective way to measure every choice we make. When we live for something greater than ourselves, we have the meaning, the motive, and the momentum to live for the ultimate instead of settling for the immediate.

Popular speaker and author, Jay Strack, advises young people: "Don't sacrifice your future on the altar of the immediate." Our future isn't about acquiring more prestige, bigger thrills, or the latest technology. A goal worth pursuing is always about changing lives. The other things may look attractive now, but someday we will regret the time we wasted on them. Success isn't measured by the money we make or the recognition we receive, but by the lives we touch and the impact we have.

Jackie Robinson broke the color barrier in Major League Baseball. From the beginning, he knew he wasn't playing only for himself. His courage opened the door of opportunity for millions of people in every aspect of American life. He later reflected, "A life is not important except in the impact it has on other lives."[37]

Some people live for the moment simply because the present is all they think about. Others are so discouraged by failure that they give up on their hopes to make something magnificent of their lives. Each of us is completely convinced that our choices make perfect sense—even the dumbest ones. We don't realize that living for the immediate is ruining our lives. We think it's the ticket to real happiness!

Don't settle for a meaningless life. Be bold. Try something you've never attempted before. Live a life that demands an explanation. If you want to change the world, you'll probably have to break some rules. Remember, Wilbur and Orville Wright never had a pilot's license. Don't let people discourage you. Listen to others and value their input, but don't let their skepticism affect your hopes. Many of your friends won't make

> Live a life that demands an explanation.

similar exchanges, but maybe you can find one or two who have a sense of adventure and will go with you. If not, launch out alone.

No matter how many times you have tried and failed, try something else. It's never too late to start over. You may be discouraged, and you may feel stuck in a rut. Find the courage to stand up and try again. Never give up. Do things now that most people won't in order to spend the rest of your life accomplishing things most people can't.

LOOKING BACK, LOOKING FORWARD

I recently needed to prepare a talk to high school students, so I decided to dig through my old stuff at my parents' house and look through my yearbooks. I wanted to remember what I experienced during those years. What had I been thinking? What were my hopes, and what were my struggles? People see me now as I travel, lead, and speak, but they have no idea that I wasn't always the kid voted "most likely to succeed."

I opened the yearbook from the eighth grade and found a note from one of my teachers. (I know. I must not have been very cool if I had my teachers writing in my yearbook.) Mrs. Wingate wrote, "Kevin, if you ever realize your full potential and actually apply yourself, there will be no stopping you." She was exactly right. I had some potential, but I did as little as possible to get by. Her words were very kind . . . sort of painful . . . and right on target.

One time in middle school I walked by a classroom full of kids. I smiled and waved to them, but I only used one of my fingers. I wasn't angry, and I wasn't trying to be a smart aleck. I was just trying to be funny and cool—but the teacher was not amused! I got in-school suspension.

In my last year of high school, I turned in a paper. As always, I had tried to skate by with as little work as possible. When I got it back, my teacher had given me a really bad grade. I always thought I could talk my way out of any situation, so I walked up to the front to have a private talk with her. I kind of laughed and said, "I know this isn't my best work, but I know I did better than the kid sitting next to me, and he got a better grade."

The teacher knew I was asking her to change my grade. She didn't hesitate. She said calmly and clearly, "Kevin, I'm not measuring you against any other student. I'm measuring you against what you're capable of doing. This wasn't close to your capability. Do you understand?"

I didn't like it, but I understood.

Reflecting back on those years was helpful in gaining some perspective. I was never the class valedictorian, I wasn't a star athlete, and I wasn't our class president. I did, however, have untapped potential.

Mrs. Wingate's inscription in my yearbook, the suspension, and the honest comment about not giving my best were all wakeup calls for me. They pushed me to realize I was capable of more. In the same way, I hope this book pushes you to evaluate your life and reach farther than you ever have before.

Some who are reading this book have made straight A's in school, and some would have been happy just to make a B once in a while. Some come from affluent families, but others are barely scraping by. Some have stable, happy homes, but others live with painful memories of abuse, addiction, and abandonment. Some already know how they want to invest their lives, but many are still searching.

Everyone has a purpose for his or her life. Your family, teachers, bosses, and friends may expect a lot from you. If not, it's up to you to generate your own motivation. In my case, the middle schooler who tried to get a laugh by using his middle finger finally found something big to live for. During all those years in school, my mother may have thought I would make something of my life, but not everyone else did . . . including me. Yet in the past few years I have had the privilege of working with leaders on six continents and from more than 100 countries. If making the exchanges enabled me to find a life worth living, they can help you, too.

No matter where you've been or what you've done, you have wonderful opportunities ahead of you. The door to it may seem hidden right now,

> No matter where you've been or what you've done, you have wonderful opportunities ahead of you. The door to it may seem hidden right now, but it's there.

but it's there. Don't just close this book and put it on a shelf. You won't be able to make all the exchanges at once, but you can make at least one right now. You can make a decision to swap immediate comfort for ultimate meaning. Whatever you do, do something!

- Get involved.
- Close the laptop and make the phone call.
- Fill out the application.
- Send your résumé and try to get the job.
- Pack the trailer and go.
- Write the note.
- Offer to help.
- Don't wait to be asked.
- Take the risk.
- Be fully present.
- Focus on excellence.
- Ask for greater faith and courage.
- Face the flak.
- Make the payment.
- Set up the appointment.
- Have the honest conversation.
- Turn off the game.
- Get up and make a human connection.
- Narrow the options.
- Make a choice.

Do it now.

You can't change your past, but you can change your future. You won't change it, though, by settling for the way things have always been.

Exchanges require clear thinking and a courageous heart. Which exchange resonates with you? Start there. No rationalization, no delays, and no excuses. You aren't a product of your circumstances; you're a product of your choices. Make a commitment right now, and take action immediately. It doesn't have to be perfect—in fact, I can almost guarantee that it won't be—but do it anyway. The first step is the most important one. Take it. It's the first step of the adventure of your life.

> *"I have been impressed with the urgency of doing. Knowing is not enough; we must apply. Being willing is not enough, we must do."*
> —*Leonardo da Vinci*

THINK ABOUT IT . . .

What are some reasons why immediate gratification is so appealing? What are the dangers of living for it?

What are three specific ways you can invest in having an ultimate impact on others?

As you think about the eight exchanges, which was most meaningful to you? Explain your answer.

What is your next step? When will you take it? How will it impact your life?

ENDNOTES

1   Cited at www.creators.com/opinion/mark-shields/what-joseph-heller-could-teach-wall-street.html © 2009 Mark Shields

2   Cited in the *New World Encyclopedia,* www.newworldencyclopedia.org/entry/John_D._Rockefeller

3   Donald Miller, *A Million Miles in a Thousand Years* (Nashville: Thomas Nelson, 2011), p. 108.

4   Jack Johnson, Anthony Cornelius Hamilton, & Mark Christopher Batson, "The News," © 2000 Songs of Universal Inc., Bat Future Music, Tappy Whyte's Music, Bubble Toes Publishing

5   Cited at www.outreachmagazine.com/features/4897-becoming-a-church-of-grace-and-truth.html?p=4

6   Shauna Niequist, "Instagram's Envy Effect," *Relevant,* April 4, 2013. www.relevantmagazine.com/culture/tech/stop-instagramming-your-perfect-life

7   Linda Stone. "Continuous Partial Attention," cited at lindastone.net/qa/continuous-partial-attention/

8   C.S. Lewis, *The Four Loves* (New York: Houghton Mifflin Harcourt, 1991), p. 65.

9   "Bubba Watson taking time off," ESPN Golf, May 3, 2012, cited at espn.go.com/golf/story/_/id/7886862/bubba-watson-announces-skip-players-championship-take-month-off

10 Lewis Smedes, *Forgive and Forget,* (San Francisco: HarperCollins, 1996), p. 79.

11 Dave Feinleib, "Why Startups Fail," Forbes, November 13, 2012, www.forbes.com/sites/davefeinleib/2012/11/13/why-startups-fail-2/

12 *Congressional Record: Proceedings and Debates of the 107th Congress,* p. 11,310.

13 Many excellent money management books are available, including several by Dave Ramsey and Clark Howard.

14 Cited by Richard Stearns, *The Hole in Our Gospel* (Nashville: Thomas Nelson, 2009), p. 9.

15 "25 Years: The MECTIZAN Donation Program," www.merck.com/about/featured-stories/mectizan1.html

16 Dr. Les Parrott, *Control Freak* (Carol Stream, Illinois: Tyndale House Publishers, 2000), p. 10.

17 John Mark Hall / Hector Alonzo Cervantes, Lyrics © Sony/ATV Music Publishing LLC, 2003

18   Larry Crabb, *Finding God,* (Grand Rapids: Zondervan, 1993), p. 18.

19   M. Scott Peck, *The Road Less Traveled* (New York: Simon & Schuster, 1978), p. 15.

20   *60 Minutes,* November 6, 2005.

21   Cited by Ted Bernard in *Hope and Hard Times: Communities, Collaboration and Sustainability* (Gabriola Island, Canada: New Society Publishers, 2010), p. 11.

22   Malcolm Gladwell, *Outliers: The Story of Success* (Back Bay Books, 2011).

23   Adapted from "Vocation: Discerning Your Calling," Dr. Tim Keller, © 2011 by Redeemer City to City, cdn.theresurgence.com/files/2011/06/06/Vocation-Discerning_Your_Calling.pdf.

24   E. B. White and Martha White, *In the Words of E.B. White* (Ithaca, New York: Cornell University Press, 2011), p. 148.

25   I recommend the DiSC Behavioral Assessment. Other useful tools are the StrengthsFinder, the Myers-Briggs Type Indicator, and the Birkman Method.

26   "Think Different," Apple video presentation, 1997, Richard Dreyfuss narration.

27   Quoted in *Coco Chanel: Her Life, Her Secrets,* by Marcel Haedrich, 1971.

28   Cited in *Quotes about Leaders and Leadership,* quotationsbook.com, p. 6.

29   Seth Godin, *Purple Cow* (New York: Portfolio, 2003), p. 45.

30   Steven Furtick, *Sun Stand Still* (Multnomah Books: Colorado Springs, 2010), p. 91.

31   Cited by Gary McGuire, *Secrets of Successful People* (Epitome Books, 2009), p. 94.

32   Billy Graham, "A Time for Moral Courage," *Reader's Digest,* July 1964.

33   "Remarks on East-West Relations at the Brandenburg Gate in West Berlin." Ronald Reagan Presidential Library, www.reagan.utexas.edu/archives/speeches/1987/061287d.htm.

34   Cited by Bob Weinstein, Lt. Col. Bob Weinstein, Ken Blanchard, et al in *Discover Your Inner Strength* (Health Colonel Publishing: Ft. Lauderdale, 2009), p. 233.

35   Jenna Goudreau, "Why We Need to Take 20-Somethings Seriously," *Forbes,* April 24, 2012, www.forbes.com/sites/jennagoudreau/2012/04/24/why-we-need-to-take-20-somethings-seriously/

36   "Top five regrets of dying," *The Guardian,* February 1, 2012, www.theguardian.com/lifeandstyle/2012/feb/01/top-five-regrets-of-the-dying?view=mobile

37   Joseph Dorinson and Joram Warmund, *Jackie Robinson: Race, Sports, and the American Dream* (Armonk, New York: M.E. Sharpe, Inc., 1999), p. 207.

Acknowledgements

This book simply wouldn't have happened without the support, advice, and encouragement of many people. In particular, I want to thank . . .

. . . Garrett Gravesen, my best friend and business partner, who always reminds me, "If it's not WOW, it's not worth doing!"

. . . Pat Springle, for helping put into words what I have wanted to communicate so long. Along with your help through this process, your encouragement has meant the world.

. . . My parents, for making sacrifices, believing in me, and teaching me what's most important in life.

. . . My adopted grandparents, Andy and Carolyn Smith, for coming into my life, filling a void, and making me their own grandson.

. . . My sister Whitney, for being the younger—yet often wiser—sibling. Thanks for keeping me grounded.

. . . And my uncle, known by my friends as "Cool Uncle Mark," for his timely advice.

For your assistance during the *8 Essential Exchanges* journey, thanks to Lindsay and Justin Miller, Kristin King, Candace and Phil Wilkes, John Hightower, and the Decycive team.

I'd also like to thank people who have believed in me and model the importance of making exchanges that matter. These people include Vince and Barbara Dooley, Ike Reighard, Coach Mark Richt, Jennifer

Kilcrease, Jere Morehead, Todd Williams, the Leaders Lyceum family, and the great folks at Chick-fil-A, including Rodney Bullard, Mark Miller, David Salyers, L.J. Yankosky, Lauren Thigpen, and the Cathy family.

The ADDO dream would not have come true without people and organizations that helped us from the beginning. Thanks to Wayne Collett, Steve Crowley, Donna Monroe, Laura Holder, Heath Garrett, Bert Reeves, Aaron Harris, the Teague family and Walton Communities, Brad Respess and Tip Top Poultry, as well as the great team at Cobb County Schools, including Cheryl Hungerford, John Stafford, Billy Richardson, and others. Also, I'm very thankful for the ADDO Institute Board: Josh Paradis, Matt Elliott, and David Nicholas.

A number of people have encouraged (and prodded) me along the way, including Jackie Hubert, Laura Burch, Earl Leonard, Drew Fulton, Grant and Brie Zarzour, Tyler Jacobs, Danny Prince, Brooks Bradway, Ellis Edwards, Lindsey Parker, Mike Linch, Johnny and Judy Foster, Nathan Galloway, Greg Carter, Travis Pierce, Margaret Wingate, Roger Hines, Andrew Dill, Jon Barker, Kathleen Bennett, Alysse Whatley, the entire UGA HEROs crew, and my Eastwood church family.

Finally, I want to acknowledge the impact of those who have inspired me on my journeys abroad, especially Paulus in Indonesia, Nicholas in South Africa, Paula in Romania, and Madelein in Colombia.

To all of you, I am profoundly grateful.

About the Author

Kevin Paul Scott has traveled to six continents and spoken to leaders from more than 100 countries. Kevin co-founded both ADDO Worldwide and the ADDO Institute. The ADDO Institute received the Governor's International Award for "New Company of the Year" in the state of Georgia. The Institute works specifically in the areas of global leadership, student leadership and thought leadership.

Prior to founding ADDO, Kevin's background included non-profit charitable work, business ventures, and politics. After graduating from the University of Georgia, Kevin served on a presidential campaign team and then worked as a representative for a United States Congressman.

Kevin was named one of the "Power 30 Under 30" for his work in expanding the marketing efforts nationwide as the Communicator in Chief for a global company. In consecutive years, Kevin was named to the "40 under 40" lists for Georgia Trend and then the Atlanta Business Chronicle.

For his leadership and business acumen, Kevin has been featured on Fox Business, CNBC, CNN, and in numerous publications, including The New York Times, Washington Post, Los Angeles Times, Atlanta Journal Constitution, Detroit Free Press, The Economist and others.

For fun, Kevin has been cage diving with Great White Sharks in South Africa, trekked Mountain Gorillas in Uganda, and rode a llama in Colombia. However, he most enjoys being at home to cheer on the Atlanta Braves and Georgia Bulldogs. Kevin was raised in Kennesaw, GA and is active in his local church. Kevin is the co-author of *The Lepers' Lessons: Five Questions, Two Perspectives, and the Pursuit of Purpose.* Kevin speaks extensively at businesses, universities and within the faith community.

Learn more at KevinPaulScott.com

About ADDO

ADDO Worldwide

ADDO is a brand + experience consultancy. ADDO helps businesses and brands ideate and activate initiatives to enhance leadership and social impact. ADDO creates ways for companies to maximize "doing business" while "doing good" to deliver tangible, sustainable and measurable engagement with customers and their communities.

ADDO Worldwide consults on strategic business initiatives, communication strategies, and effective employee engagement. In partnership with Chick-fil-A, ADDO Worldwide has created a high school leadership program: Chick-fil-A Leader Academy. The innovative program teaches project-based leadership and emphasizes "impact through action."

ADDO Institute

ADDO Institute is a 501(c)(3) not-for-profit organization that engages individuals of all ages through leadership development and cultural travel.

The ADDO Institute received the Governor's International Award for "New Company of the Year" in the State of Georgia.

For more information, go to www.addo.is

ADDO Founders, Kevin and Garrett, with former Secretaries of State
Colin Powell, James Baker, Warren Christopher, Madeleine Albright and
Henry Kissinger.